# A Beginners' Guide
to the
## Dolls' House Hobby

# A Beginners' Guide
## to the
# Dolls' House Hobby

## JEAN NISBETT

**GUILD OF MASTER CRAFTSMAN PUBLICATIONS**

First published 1997 by
Guild of Master Craftsman Publications Ltd,
166 High Street, Lewes,
East Sussex BN7 1XU

Reprinted 1997

ISBN 1 86108 037 9

**Principal photography by Alec Nisbett**
(Other photographs as acknowledged below)

Line drawings by John Yates

Designed by Teresa Dearlove

Typeface: Garamond

Printed in Hong Kong by H & Y Printing Ltd
Colour separation by Viscan Graphics, Singapore

**Photo acknowledgements**
Jean Nisbett and the Guild of Master Craftsman Publications gratefully acknowledge the following people
and agencies for granting permission to reproduce their photographs in this book. The photographs on
the following pages were supplied courtesy of: Anglesey Dolls' Houses p.41; Carol Black Miniatures p..22
(bottom right); Alan Borwell of Borcraft Miniatures p.38 (top); Mrs G Brookes of Honeychurch Toys Ltd
pp.7 (top left), 9 (top left), 17 (bottom right), 21 (left), 29 (right), 48; Hugh Cason of Warren Dolls' Houses
p.7 (bottom); Jeremy Collins of Gable End Designs p.18 (top right); Trevor and Sue Cook p.69 (top); Martin
and Tricia Dare of Lilydale Designs p.33 (bottom; photograph by Gordon Rossiter); Dolls' House Emporium
p.34 (right); Dragonfly Designs p.75 (top right); Greenleaf Products, Inc. pp.7 (top right),
71 (right); E A Groocock of the Miniature Display Company p.28; Robert Longstaff Workshops p.36 (left);
Carol Mann p.32 (top right; photograph by Maggy Milner); James Parker of Elphin Homes p.8;
Ann Shepley p.23 (top right and bottom); Sid Cooke Dolls' Houses pp.6 (right), 40; Georgina Steeds p.31
(left; photograph by Liz Eddison/New Shoots); Keith Thorne pp.33 (top left), 73, 75 (centre right);
Tridias Ltd p.34 (left); Trevor Webster of Vale Dolls' Houses p.107 (top left).

On the front cover: gazebo (top left) by Keith Thorne; Aga oven (centre bottom) by Gable End Designs;
house (bottom right) by Elphin Homes. On the back cover: 'Edwards' shop by Anglesey Dolls' Houses.

**Measurements**
Although care has been taken to ensure that metric measurements are true and accurate, they are only
conversions from imperial. Throughout the book instances may be found where an imperial measurement
has slightly varying metric equivalents, usually within 0.5mm either way, because in each particular case
the closest metric equivalent has been given. Care should be taken to use either imperial or metric
measurements consistently. (*See* also Metric Conversion Table, page 114.)

**For
Jake, Oliver,
Martha and Millie**

# Contents

# Acknowledgements

I would like to thank my editor, Elizabeth Inman, for her initial idea and her enthusiastic approach, and Bryony Bénier for keeping everything on schedule; my husband, Alec, for sparing time from his filming schedule for photography: without him this book would not have been possible; Caroline Nisbett and Ian Middleton for providing the design and typography to complete my dolls' house shop facade; Guy Nisbett for creating the Japanese garden setting.

Thanks are due to the following miniaturists, whose work appears in the photographs:

Wendy Allin (shell tray p.102); Anglesey Dolls' Houses ('Edwards' shop p.28 and 'Victoria House' p.41); Reuben Barrows (fibreglass sheets pp.55 and 71); Tom Batt (miniature oil painting p.79); Bishopstoke Miniatures ('marble'-topped side table p.95); Carol Black Miniatures (patchwork quilts p.22); Black Country Miniatures (leaded lights and fanlight on 'Victoria House' p.41 and shop p.103); Borcraft Miniatures (Christmas room p.38, wooden mouldings and pediment p.62, picture frame mouldings p.96); Cairn Tiles (slates and chimney p.72); Christopher Cole (small-scale Georgian house p.4, green shop front p.46); Trevor and Sue Cook (ceiling rose p.24, Chinese room p.69); Terry Curran (flagstones pp.32 and 77, tiles on corner fireplace p.52, Roman tiles p.72); Dolls' House Emporium ('Blossom Cottage' p.34); Domat Designs (house p.35); Dragonfly Designs (gatehouse porch p.75); Escutcheon (lyre-end sofa table p.26); Gable End Designs (double-oven Aga p.18); Greenleaf Products Inc. (dolls' houses pp.7 and 71); Honeychurch Toys Ltd (dolls' houses pp.7, 9, 17, 21, 48, also my interior design shop – kit supplied by Small Sorts, Salisbury, carpets by Mini Marvels – pp.30, 42, 103); Muriel Hopwood (Art Deco plates p.61, Chinese vase p.84); Sadie Joscelyne (china leopards p.95); Lilydale Designs (lean-to, rabbit hutch and shed p.33); Dora Lockyer (mattress p.22); Carol Lodder (Dutch tulip vase and flower brick pp.52 and 99, pink spongeware pp.61 and 97); Terry McAlister (butter churn p.25, pot crane and spit p.77); Carol Mann (garden pots p.32); Nicola Mascall Miniatures (bell pull p.99); Peter Mattinson (Mackintosh wall plaque p.26, plaster roundel p.52, classical bust p.95); Merry Gourmet Miniatures (food p.16, patio p.31, flower arrangements p.32, garden setting p.105); Miniature Display Company (display in 'Edwards' shop p.28); Jane Newman (pine bathroom furniture p.23); Phoenix Metal Kits (grate p.97); Colin and Yvonne Roberson (metal bed p.22, period perambulator p.29, cradle p.93); Gordon Rossiter (Tudor chimney p.75); Helen Scott-Langley (miniature painting of 'Spring' p.96); Ann Shepley (bathrooms p.23, kitchen tiles pp.17 and 77); Sid Cooke Dolls' Houses (dolls' houses pp.6 and 40); Georgina Steeds (garden setting for conservatory p.31); Stillmore Homes (oriental garden building p.108); Stokesay Ware (jardiniere p.100); Sussex Crafts (resin floor tiles p.24); Tetbury Miniatures (sofa/armchair kit p.21); Keith Thorne (dolls' houses pp.33, 73, 75); Bernardo Traettino (window p.45); Tridias Ltd (children's open plan dolls' house p.34); Vale Dolls' Houses (ready-built conservatory p.107); Warren Dolls' Houses (stacking kit dolls' house p.7); Valerie Warren (wooden-headed dolls p.37); John Watkins (house and miniature wrought-iron work pp.2 and 9, metal roof ridging p.107, weather-vane p.74); Doug Woodyard (dairy cart p.25, loaned for photography by Caroline Nevill Miniatures); the Art Gallery (p.30) was also loaned for photography by Caroline Nevill Miniatures.

# Introduction

There is something for everyone in the dolls' house hobby. Now a popular adult pastime in many countries, children can also be involved. Dolls' houses appeal to people with a wide range of interests, and the woodworker, the interior decorator, the artist and the needle-worker can all find scope for their talents in this absorbing miniature world.

In the early 1980s the dolls' house hobby was just beginning to take off in Britain, although it was already well established in America. At that time I was happily restoring old dolls' houses that I had found in junk shops and a local street market. I taught myself

**A collector's dolls' house, arranged as a series of room sets rather than the more usual home. Six good-sized rooms and deep recesses in the front-opening doors allow plenty of space to display a variety of miniatures. A panel in the roof lifts off to reveal a loft.**

how to repair damaged woodwork, found out by trial and error which paints looked best on small-scale dwellings, and experimented with a variety of materials to make attractive flooring.

Occasionally someone would come along with a better class of house which they wanted me to decorate in period style. It was a short step from the renovation of old houses to the interior design and decoration of new, craftsman-made 1/12-scale dolls' houses. Today, still, nothing gives me a more pleasurable feeling of anticipation than a plain wooden house, waiting to be transformed into a desirable residence.

Now that dolls' houses are so popular as a hobby for grown-ups, it is all much easier. Everything you could possibly want for your dolls' house is readily available in the internationally accepted 1/12 scale, including period-style wooden mouldings, doors and windows which can be assembled from kits, and flooring materials ranging from easy-to-cut sheets to individual Victorian tiles. These accessories can be mass-produced and inexpensive, or the sought-after work of specialist craftspeople.

If you are just starting out, this book will introduce you to the dolls' house hobby, showing a clear path through the confusion of choices. It will help you to decide what sort of dolls' house you really want, whether to make it from a kit or buy one ready-made, where to obtain everything you need and the level of costs involved.

Part One will give you an overview of what is available and the decisions you need to make, while Part Two offers all the practical advice and information you will need to get started. I have included tried-and-tested ideas for making furnishings and accessories, sometimes from the most surprising materials, as well as step-by-step instructions with easy-to-follow diagrams for fixtures and fittings. Once you begin, you are sure to think of many new ideas yourself.

Assembling furniture from kits is popular, and to help you achieve good results I have included some guidance which you may not find in the maker's instructions.

The most charming dolls' houses generally contain a mixture of bought and home-made furnishings, just like a real home. Whether you decide to make or buy most of the contents, I am sure that you will enjoy every minute as you decorate and furnish a miniature home that will continue to delight you and your family for years to come. This book will help you to avoid expensive mistakes, save time trying to solve frustrating problems, and gain maximum enjoyment from a truly rewarding hobby.

**A desirable residence: a scale model of an early Victorian home.**

# Part
# One
# *Planning*

# 1 *Starting out*

## Scale

The first thing you need to know is that most dolls' houses and their contents are made to a standard scale of 1/12. One inch represents 12in, therefore, and 1cm represents 12cm. Although 12 is not a 'metric' number, these measurements are used internationally.

## Examples of 1/12-scale measurements

To help you visualize how small everything will be, some sample dimensions are given below. These measurements are the most common, but there will be some variation, particularly in the size of dolls' house rooms.

**Rooms**
| | |
|---|---|
| Depth | 9½ to 10½in (24.2 to 26.7cm) |
| Ceiling height | 9 to 11in (22.9 to 27.9cm) |
| Width of room | 9½ to 10½in (24.2 to 26.7cm) |

**Furniture**
| | |
|---|---|
| Wardrobe | Height 6½in (16.5cm) |
| Fourposter bed | Height 6½in (16.5cm) |
| | Length 6in (15.2cm) |
| | Width 5in (12.7cm) |
| Single bed | Length 6½in (16.5cm) |
| | Width 3in (7.6cm) |
| Double bed | Width 5in (12.7cm) |
| Dining chair | Height of seat 1½in (3.8cm) |
| | Total height 3in (7.6cm) |
| Armchair/sofa | Height of seat 1¼in (3.2cm) |
| | Height of back varies |

| | |
|---|---|
| Dining table | Height 2½in (6.4cm) |
| | Length and width varies |

**Dolls**
| | |
|---|---|
| Gentleman | Height 6in (15.2cm) |
| Lady | Height 5½in (14cm) |
| Child | Height 3 to 4in (7.6 to 10.2cm) |
| Toddler | Height 2½ to 3in (6.4 to 7.6cm) |

## Other scales

You may come across smaller scales: 1/24 or even 1/48 are made by some dedicated crafts-people, but these are more suitable for the devotee of the miniscule, with all the extra difficulties of decorating and furnishing in such a small size. It is best to choose 1/12 scale for a first dolls' house, as it will be much easier to find wallpapers, furniture and accessories in the correct size.

**This appealing Georgian house takes up little space as the scale is smaller than the more usual 1/12 scale. Most of the contents were made specially to fit the tiny rooms.**

# Choosing your dolls' house

## Aims

Before you buy your first dolls' house, think about what you want to achieve and what will give you the greatest enjoyment. What is your main interest? It may be period-style decoration and furniture, collecting miniatures, making your own contents, design and decoration, or woodwork. Who is the dolls' house for? Although many dolls' houses are equally suitable for a child or a collector, if you are specifically planning a house for a child your aims will be slightly different. (For information on dolls' houses designed for children, *see* pages 34–8.)

## Setting a budget

There is so much choice that it is wise to do some advance planning before you go out on a buying expedition. You probably know roughly how much you can spend on a dolls' house and what you are likely to be able to spend on your hobby in the future. Whether it is a small or large amount, you still need to work out your priorities. If money is no object, a dolls' house can be commissioned from one of the crafts-people who make to order, fully decorated both inside and out. For most of us, however, what we spend on our hobby is likely to be much closer to the amount a drama enthusiast might spend on theatre tickets, or a film buff on visits to the cinema.

Enjoyment of the hobby is certainly not dependent on how much you spend. Miniature interior design and decoration is something anyone can learn. Making furniture, or assembling it from kits, is rewarding in itself and you will find that you can make many attractive accessories and ornaments from inexpensive materials.

It is wise to decide first on the size of house which would suit you best. If you are a beginner on a limited budget, a two- or four-room house is a good way to start. This will allow you to gain experience before you go on to something larger. A nine-room house will cost a lot to furnish completely, even if you make many of the items yourself, but it would be an ideal ongoing project for several years. Again, it is really a question of your aims and interests.

## A room box

If space and money for your new hobby is very limited, you can create your first miniature scene in a room-box setting. It is surprising how much can be achieved with one room and a very small budget.

Room boxes are available either finished or as kits to assemble yourself. An average size is 15in long by 10in high by 9in deep (38.1cm long by 25.4cm high by 22.9cm deep), which gives plenty of space. Some are provided with a sliding Perspex front to keep out the dust. Alternatively, you could use any wooden box of a suitable size. I have even seen miniature scenes created in an old clock case.

## The time factor

You will also need to consider how much time you have to devote to your hobby. Making everything yourself, whether from accumulated bits and pieces or from kits, is time-consuming but very satisfying, while collecting gives you an excuse for excursions to minia-tures fairs and dolls' house shops. Whichever approach appeals to you, your dolls' house will evolve gradually, depending on how much time you have to spend on it.

## Research

It is always useful to gather some local infor-mation. It should be easy to locate the nearest dolls' house shop from the classified telephone directory, and any miniatures fairs in your area will be advertised in the local press. Visiting one of these fairs and having a good look around it will give you a clear idea about the range of options available. Even if you spend very little, you should come home brimming with ideas and inspiration.

### Specialist magazines

Dolls' house hobby magazines contain helpful and practical features and pictures as well as listing forthcoming miniatures fairs. You may find there are fairs that are not advertised in your local newspaper but which are still accessible. There will also be addresses for many dolls' house shops and mail order suppliers, as well as details of miniatures made by specialist craftspeople. Shops and suppliers will be able to provide the specific items mentioned in this book, and specialist magazines will be the most practical way of discovering suitable stockists. Information about dolls' house clubs will also be given. (*See* page 113 for details of British, Continental and American dolls' house magazines.)

# Price comparisons

Most moderately priced, ready-made dolls' houses are supplied undecorated and you will find a wide price range, sometimes between houses which at first glance seem similar. An inexpensive house will be provided with a basic staircase without balusters or handrail, and the rooms will be empty boxes. A more expensive model may be fitted with chimney breasts and even interior doors. You will need to balance up the amount of money available and the amount of work you want to do yourself.

## Medium density fibreboard or plywood

In general, the price will reflect not only the detailing but also the material used to make the house, and in most cases this will be either MDF (medium density fibreboard) or plywood.

**MDF** is less expensive than plywood. It has a smooth surface which takes a paint finish well. It is, however, heavier than plywood, which can be a disadvantage if you want to move a large house around.

**Plywood** can split if it is of poor quality, especially when screws have been used in assembling the house. It may also warp if placed too near a radiator for any length of time. Nonetheless, if you plan to create an antique effect and want to stain and polish, or varnish the facade of your house, then plywood is essential.

## Houses assembled from kits

A dolls' house which you can build yourself from a kit will cost around half to two-thirds the price of the same model ready-made, depending on the complexity of the design. Kits which use MDF have ready-cut slots and grooves to be fitted together and glued, which makes them easy to assemble and ideal for the beginner.

**Victoria Cottage is an inexpensive small house made of MDF with plywood trim, and is a good kit for a beginner to make up. It can also be supplied assembled. The hinged roof lifts to reveal an attic room; components include a staircase, turned balusters and window trim.**

**Varnish solved the problem of how to decorate a well-made plywood house with black lettering printed on the facade. It took eight coats of satin-finish varnish to produce a perfect result, but was well worth the effort. Coloured stain-varnish was used for the door and roof.**

An Edwardian house assembled from a plywood kit. The facade faithfully reproduces all the period details. Some experience of carpentry would be helpful in making up this type of kit, which requires screws as well as glue.

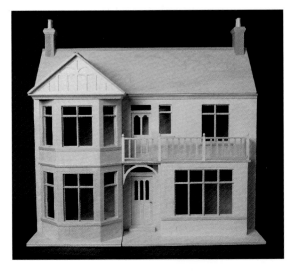

This is an ideal kit house for a beginner: the sections snap together easily and the shingles and decorative trim are glued on. Coventry Cottage has all the charming details customary of American-made dolls' houses and, as usual for these houses, is open at the back (and also one side) for ease of access.

## House extensions

Apart from price considerations, another advantage of building a house from a kit is that you can start small and extend later. Several makers provide stacking kits with optional extra storeys, so that you can start with a basic house or shop and then add additional storeys later as you wish. The roof is usually fitted with simple locating screws which can be taken out easily to add the extra storey, and the roof is then refitted on top. An alternative arrangement is an additional basement, which will raise the house by one storey (*see* page 40).

If you have some model making or woodwork experience, you will probably be able to tackle a kit house in plywood, which requires more work and involves screws as well as glue in the assembly. You will need to use some woodworking tools (*see* pages 46–7). Practical tips on assembling kits can be found on pages 40–1.

## American kit houses

Some of the larger American kits will have an astonishing number of small pieces, fairly roughly finished, and reaching a satisfactory conclusion is a little like completing a gigantic jigsaw puzzle. They look very impressive when finished, however, especially if care is taken to sand the wood smooth and fill any gaps with woodfiller before painting. It is best to start with one of the smaller models until you have gained experience.

Another good choice for the beginner: initially a kit for a one-storey house, extra storeys can be added one at a time when required. Assembly is straightforward and in addition to the instruction leaflet, the makers offer a video showing exactly how to proceed.

# 2 An introduction to period properties

Many dolls' houses are made in period styles and it is often a fascination with a particular era which draws people into the hobby in the first place. Georgian seems to be the most popular, while Tudor and Victorian are not far behind. Craftspeople make more miniature furniture from these periods because of demand, but other styles are now catching up rapidly, especially Edwardian and the 1930s and '40s. Deciding on your favourite style may be easy, but choosing a dolls' house is a little like buying a real one: you know it is right when you see it. Any plans you have made for a country cottage or Georgian town house could well be forgotten when you fall in love with a three-bedroom semi or a Gothic folly.

It is usually the exterior of the house that is the deciding factor in your choice, but it is also important to inspect the inside thoroughly.

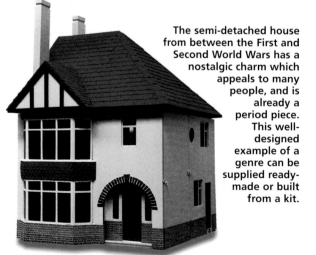

The semi-detached house from between the First and Second World Wars has a nostalgic charm which appeals to many people, and is already a period piece. This well-designed example of a genre can be supplied ready-made or built from a kit.

The exterior may be just right, but does the internal layout suit your ideas? One vital point to bear in mind is ease of access. Whatever the style of house it will, for example, be simpler to decorate if the window glazing is not fixed in before the house is painted (*see* pages 65 and 109). Removable staircases are another convenience for the dolls' house decorator; some makers fix them with slots, or an easily removable screw (*see* pages 58–9 and 61 for advice on decorating around staircases).

## Exterior decoration: co-ordinating period style and colour

Once you have chosen a house, and before you begin on the decoration, decide how you want the completed house to look. It is easy to re-wallpaper or repaint the rooms inside if you change your mind, but far more difficult to redecorate the outside successfully. The types of finish used for the exterior are tricky to remove and you may not get a perfectly smooth finish on the redecoration, especially if architectural features have also been altered.

The exterior finish can be as simple or as elaborate as you wish, but you will find that the effect is better if the colours and materials you choose are suited to the period style of the house. If possible, study some real examples. You might also look in home

The Edwardian house shown in its undecorated state on page 7 has been transformed with white paintwork on a brick-red facade. The Edwardian style borrowed a little from many previous periods and the mock half-timbering on the gable was a much admired feature.

improvement magazines dealing with the restoration of period buildings, to find examples of authentic Georgian paint colours, or to see just how an Edwardian house looked in its heyday. Even for a modern dolls' house it is worth looking at a few full-size examples, to help sort out your ideas on colour schemes.

# Degrees of detail

There are all sorts of finish you can use on the outside of your dolls' house: it all depends on how much you like messing about with paint and glue. I find great satisfaction in mixing paint colours and achieving the perfect shade I have in mind for a particular house. If you want a realistic special effect, it is possible to simulate plaster, stucco or pebble dash (*see* page 68). As with the facade, the roof can be simply painted, or it could be papered to resemble roof tiles or slates or, if you want to be more adventurous, you can go for the full treatment by adding wooden shingles or realistic ceramic tiles (*see* pages 71 and 72).

If your main interest is in the interior furnishings or in collecting miniatures, there is

no need to indulge in what might seem like hard work on the exterior. A simple, painted finish on the walls and roof in well-chosen colours might be just right.

The simple guide to suitable exterior finishes below should help you decide what will fit your needs and your particular house. Practical details on both easy and more time-consuming options are all given in Part Two (*see* pages 66–7 and 71–5).

A scaled down replica of an early Victorian house. Built in the 1830s and '40s, these houses followed the standard Georgian plan inside, without the over-elaboration which characterized later Victorian style. The balcony and railings are a fine example of miniaturized wrought-iron work.

## Architectural details

A dolls' house can have architectural details so accurate that it is almost a model of a real one, and again you can decide how far down this road you wish to go. Painted stucco, the hallmark of the Victorian town house, is easily copied in paint. In the interests of accuracy, you

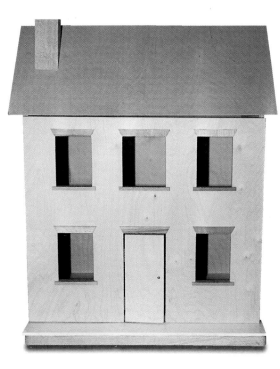

**This inexpensive house presents a neat and charming appearance with a simple paint finish picked out in white. Lace blinds at the windows add to the spick-and-span effect.**

might want to add Tuscan columns to support a portico, lintels above the windows, or perhaps pediments and architrave on the facade. Wooden bargeboards or shutters can add charm to a simple, country-style house, and quoining will enhance a plain brick one (*see* page 74). All these detailed additions are readily obtainable at reasonable prices in 1/12 scale in the form of plaster or cast resin mouldings which can be painted and then glued on.

# Historic paint colours

If you want the exterior of your dolls' house to be painted in an authentic period colour, all the help you need is at hand. Many paint manufacturers have undertaken research in this area and can provide useful shade cards in a special range of historic paint colours. In some cases paint sample pots are also available. One or two will be large enough to decorate a dolls' house. Even if no such samples are available,

you should still be able to obtain a reasonably small amount of a professional decorator paint, specially mixed, without having to go for a two-gallon (or ten-litre) can.

Some of these special colours are made only in oil-based paints or use a formula for old-fashioned distemper, and these will be more difficult to work with. To avoid this problem, it is generally better to sort through the shade cards and choose something as near as possible to your ideal from a modern range of paints. In the small scale, it will be perfectly effective. The following table is a brief guide to the colours and finishes which were commonly used in particular eras.

## Choosing shades

Look carefully at the shade card when choosing stains and varnishes. Sometimes it is better to settle for a shade which you can see is what you want, rather than be guided by the name of the finish the product is supposed to represent.

# Suitable colours and exterior finishes on period houses

| Period | | Finishes |
|---|---|---|
| Tudor/Jacobean (16th/early 17th century) | Walls | Plaster with half-timbering. White, ochre, pale pink or apricot infilling. |
| | Timbers | Stained: use walnut stain, which is warmer than light oak, to complement pale-coloured plaster. Wood stain or varnish doors and window surrounds to match. (Blackened timbers were a Victorian fashion and look striking with white plaster.) |
| | Roof | Stone tiles or simulated thatch. |
| Georgian (18th century) | Walls | Painted as stucco for a town house, using stone-coloured paint. A small Georgian cottage might be pink, pale blue or cream. |
| | Roof | Grey or russet slates, or paint. |
| | Paintwork | Pure white or 'Georgian' white (off-white) for window frames and surrounds. Dark green, black or white for front door. |
| | Railings | Today's Georgian house usually has black painted railings, but a dark bronze-green is more authentic. |
| Regency (early 19th century) | Walls | Stucco: painted finish in pale green, pale yellow, or apricot, with details picked out in white. |
| | Roof | Grey slates, or grey paint. |
| | Additions | Wedgwood plaques or plaster friezes; Greek key design frieze below cornice. |
| | Front door | Sludge green (*see* picture page 45). |
| Victorian town house (19th century) | Walls | Brick (use either printed paper, or fibreglass sheets – *see* page 55). NB: London stock brick was a pale yellow colour. Depending on the local clay, brick in other areas might have been red or a dark purple-grey. |
| | Roof | Grey slate, or grey paint. |
| | Additions | Brass door furniture and letter box. |
| | Front door | Black, or deep blue. |
| Victorian country house (19th century) | Walls | Red brick. |
| | Roof | Slate grey. |
| | Additions | Bargeboards on gable ends. A clocktower on the roof, or a turret. |
| | Front door | Dark green. |

| Edwardian (early 20th century) | Walls | Brick. |
| | Roof | Red slates, or paint (russet mix). |
| | Paintwork | White. |
| | Additions | Balcony or verandah, painted white. Mock half-timbers on gable ends. |
| | Front door | Stained as oak; stained glass panels. |
| 1930s–'40s | Walls | Brick or pebble dash. |
| | Roof | Red or grey slates. |
| | Paintwork | Mid-green. Front door could be painted mid-green, white, or stained as oak. |
| | Additions | Letter box. Stained glass panel over front door. Porch, tiled red. |
| Farmhouse | Walls | 'Sussex' pink, ochre, or white. |
| | Roof | Slate, or stone tiles. |
| | Paintwork | White, or oak timber. |
| | Front door | Stained oak or white. |
| Clapboard house English: weatherboard USA: siding | | Shaker or English eighteenth century: a Shaker house would have white clapboard; an English house might be stained dark with woodstain. |

## Window frames

On a dolls' house which has exterior walls painted or resembling brick, it always looks best to paint window frames white or off-white, which makes an attractive contrast, rather than use a darker colour which might have been used on a real house.

# Interior decoration: period or modern

Once you have come to some conclusions about the outside of your period house, you can turn your attention to the inside and let your imagination run free. First you must decide whether the house is to have period or modern room settings. It is perfectly acceptable to have up-to-date interiors in a period house, just as in real life, or you may prefer to keep everything in period. Alternatively, modern room settings mean that you can include antique furniture as well as modern items and achieve an agreeable mix. The following information outlines appropriate colours and styles for period interiors. More specific details on particular rooms can be found in Chapter 3.

# Plan your colour schemes

When you have made a choice about the style of the rooms, you can start thinking about colour. Remember that when you look into the dolls' house you will see all the rooms at once, so it makes sense to co-ordinate your schemes to some extent to avoid clashing colours in adjacent rooms. You want to strike a happy medium, as an all-pastel arrangement might look insipid, while very strong colours will dominate the scene too much. The following table offers guidelines on appropriate decoration styles for specific periods. There is always scope for imagination and alternatives, but the information here will give you the basics.

## Ceilings

Ceilings painted off-white look best in a dolls' house of any period, as they reflect soft light into the room.

# Suitable colours and materials for period interiors

| Period | | Colours/Materials |
|---|---|---|
| Tudor/Jacobean (16th/early 17th century) | Walls | Colour-washed in ochre, white or terracotta, or oak panelling (light or dark). |
| | Ceilings | Oak beams (light or dark). Beams can be stained or painted in a decorative pattern of red, green and gold (*see* pages 1 and 19). |
| | Floors | Flagstones or oak planking. |
| | Features | Large open fireplace of stone or brick, or plastered; logs arranged in an iron basket or on firedogs. Inglenook fireplace for a cottage. Planked doors and stencilled decoration. |
| Georgian (18th century) | Walls | Paint colours were limited: stone colours, drab and mouse (a sort of fawn or grey); pea green or pearl for the best rooms. |
| | Wainscotting | Painted panelling below the dado rail. |
| | Doors | Often painted dark brown or deep red. |
| Late Georgian (1780–1810) | Walls | Robert Adam-style colours: pink, green, blue and white, highlighted with gold for a grand effect; or wallpaper (including flock). |
| | Ceilings | White. |
| | Floors | Planking, not highly polished (*see* page 79). |
| | Additions | Plaster cornices; deep skirtings; pediments over doors (*see* page 62). |
| | Details | Dado rail. Adam-style fireplace for grand rooms, or simple hob grate for a small house. Six-panelled doors. |
| Regency (early 19th century) | Walls | Wallpaper, or Chinese-style decoration (*see* pages 69 and 95). |
| | Ceilings | White. |
| | Floors | Planking, as above. |
| | Features | Elaborately draped curtains; striped fabrics (bright acid yellow was very popular), or simple white muslin. Gilded mirrors and candles in wall sconces. |
| Early Victorian (1837–1880) | | A light and pretty style which gradually became darker and heavier. Fitted carpet became standard (*see* page 20). |
| Late Victorian (1880–1901) | Ceilings | White. |
| | Features | Elaborate fireplaces, in marble or faux-marble (*see* pages 49 and 50). Curtains – velvet or heavy silk with inner lace curtains – and blinds. |

| | | |
|---|---|---|
| Late Victorian *continued* | Additions | Clutter: footstools, occasional tables, workboxes, firescreens. Draped tables (*see* pages 90–1). Four-panelled doors. |
| William Morris Style (late 19th century) | | Based on medieval ideas. |
| | Walls | William Morris wallpaper designs are available in 1/12 scale, or you can use giftwrap based on his designs. |
| | Curtains | Use Liberty dress materials in Morris designs. |
| | Ceilings and paintwork | White. |
| | Flooring | Planked, light oak. |
| | Additions | Plate rack or picture rail. Carpets: Oriental or Art Nouveau. |
| Charles Rennie Mackintosh Style (early 20th century) | Walls and ceilings | White. |
| | Flooring | Plain, pale carpeting. |
| | Paintwork | White; occasionally very dark, almost black, but white looks better in dolls' houses. |
| | Features | Gesso (plaster) wall plaques (*see* picture page 26). High-backed chairs essential. Stained glass where possible (e.g. light fittings, door panels). Stencilled motifs in stylized rose design. |
| Edwardian (early 20th century) | Walls | Patterned wallpapers, (often floral), borders, panelling and deep friezes were all popular. A picture rail with a border below and a frieze above was often used (*see* page 68). |
| | Flooring | Polished wooden floor or linoleum surround, with carpet square. |
| | Paintwork | White or stained medium oak. |
| | Additions | Mirror above fireplace. Stained glass panels in front door. Grate with tiled surround and elaborate mantelshelf, sometimes incorporating shelves on either side. |
| 1930s–'40s | Kitchens | Green and cream was standard, with half-tiled walls. |
| | Bedrooms | Often pink. |
| | Lounge | Cream-washed walls with green, fawn or floral soft furnishings or, for the wealthy, an entirely pale room in shades of white and cream. |
| | Floors | Quarry tiles in the kitchen. Carpet square (patterned) with wood-grained floor surround in medium oak. |
| | Accessories | Standard lamps; hearthrug; companion set (poker, tongs and hearthbrush on a brass stand); wall lights in Art Deco style; silk or velvet cushions; flying ducks on the wall; bronze statuette in Art Deco style. |
| | Paintwork | Cream or wood-grained finish. |

# 3 *Planning the interior*

## Choosing the rooms

After you have decided what period your house will be, whether an older style or up to date, it is time to decide which rooms you would like to include. Space is at a premium in a small dolls' house, but if you have more than three rooms at your disposal you can go beyond the usual living room, kitchen and bedroom which will probably appear in one form or another, whatever the period of your house.

This is your chance to be an interior designer without the constraints imposed by a real house, where certain rooms, such as the kitchen and bathroom, will be plumbed for water, perhaps tiled, and not easily interchangeable. With a dolls' house you can choose whether you would prefer to have a large kitchen and a small, cosy living room or vice versa, depending on how you visualize your completed house, and what types of furniture and decoration appeal to you.

### Design considerations

If you want to create a complete period dolls' house, the architectural style will be carried through to the design and arrangement of the room. A modern interior would be more flexible even if you have a period exterior, because you can decide exactly how much will have been 'updated'. You might, for example, want to site a radiator on one of the walls rather than have an open fireplace.

Be cautious about mixing too many styles of period furniture with modern. Choose a few pieces of Tudor, Regency or Victorian, depending on your preference, but try to keep to one additional period style, or the result will look messy.

To give an idea of what is involved in the interior decoration of a whole dolls' house, specific suggestions for a variety of rooms follow. You may wish to refer back to the quick-reference interior decoration table on pages 13–14. Practical instructions for some of the main items mentioned below can be found in Part Two.

## Kitchen planning

For many people their favourite room in a dolls' house is the kitchen, especially if it is in an older style. Now that we have microwave ovens that work at the touch of a switch and much of the guesswork has been taken out of cooking, we seem all the more fascinated by how things were done in the past. We may not want to go back to those days in real life, but it can be great fun to recreate old-fashioned kitchens in 1/12 scale.

### Tudor or Jacobean kitchen

All cooking was done over an open fire, so an inglenook is essential. An inglenook is a large, open fireplace and the top is formed by the insertion of a long, heavy beam. A 1/12-scale version is simple to construct (*see* page 77) and it should be made first, before you decorate, as it can take up a whole wall.

Cooking utensils were rudimentary in those days. There would have been a metal rod over the fire, with a cauldron or two suspended from hooks (*see* page 53 for instructions on how to make a realistic-looking fire). Joints of meat or game could be hung from the ceiling, and there should be a cupboard for bread. Washing-up arrangements do not present a problem in the Tudor dolls' house: the pump was outside and plates were simply wiped clean after use.

# Georgian and Regency kitchen

Georgian kitchens also had few aids for the cook. All water still had to be brought in from outside, so each kitchen would have a bucket. Food needed to be kept out of the reach of mice, so shelves and high cupboards are essential. To add a busy, lived-in look, the kitchen can be festooned with ladles, spoons, blackened saucepans, a kettle suspended over the fire and a jack (to turn the spit) for cooking meat.

**A gourmet's delight: these elaborate tiered arrangements are worthy of Mrs Beeton and would make a superb centrepiece for the Georgian or Victorian table.**

# Victorian kitchen

The Victorian kitchen seems to be the most popular with dolls' house enthusiasts. There are so many tiny items that can be included – cooking utensils and gadgets, copper saucepans, food both fresh and cooked,

**This Victorian kitchen is one of my favourite rooms. There is always enough space left to fit in one more culinary treat or kitchen gadget.**

baskets of vegetables, bowls, jugs and basins. I counted 145 items in my Victorian kitchen at the last check. The only limit is the amount of space you have available, but as much as possible can be crammed in to good effect.

The nineteenth century saw the beginnings of modern plumbing, and a Victorian kitchen can include a ceramic Belfast sink and a wooden draining board, with perhaps a wooden plate rack above it.

The range is a vital focus point and can be built in very easily (*see* pages 76–7), with space at the side for a coal scuttle, and a wide mantelshelf for ornaments. In addition to the range, you will probably want to include a dresser, so that the shelves can be filled with crockery and other utensils. You will need to give some thought to the room's layout, however, because both the range and the dresser look best viewed from the front. Unless your kitchen has one long wall at the back, one or the other is going to have to fit against a side wall. I have arranged dolls' house kitchens in both ways and think that, in general, the range looks best on the back wall. If you then place the dresser fairly near to the front of the house on a side wall, you will find that its well-filled shelves can be clearly seen.

A dresser is eye-catching: here a random selection of pottery has gradually accumulated and looks as attractive as a matching set.

Most dolls' house kitchens are small, and are likely to be deep and relatively narrow. The proportions of the room are improved if the range is set against the back wall and a chimney breast the full width of the kitchen is brought forward about 1½in (3.8cm) from the back wall. The space behind this new upper section of wall is an open chimney above the range. (The same method applies when constructing an inglenook fireplace, *see* page 77.)

Sometimes an entire room can be fitted into a minute space. This evocative Edwardian scullery relies for its impact on a few items, beautifully arranged in the deep, recessed front of the Edwardian house shown earlier (*see* page 9).

The range in this late Victorian kitchen has been set into a tiled surround. The patterned tiles are replicas of the work of nineteenth-century designer William De Morgan: here they are interspersed with plain green tiles to good effect.

## 1930s–'40s kitchen

In the late 1920s and early 1930s, kitchens changed radically with the beginning of the servantless society. For many wealthy ladies this was the first time they had to think about cooking and it is surprising how much more convenient kitchens became. *Vogue* magazine even published articles on how to make sandwiches and prepare simple meals, which may seem laughable to us today but at the time must have been extremely helpful for those with no culinary knowledge.

The Aga cooker arrived on the scene in 1929 and almost immediately became a status symbol, as it still is today. You might like to fit one into your early twentieth-century kitchen, either a ready-made model or one you have constructed yourself (*see* pages 85–6).

This large double-oven Aga will look impressive if your kitchen is spacious enough to take it. It is available finished or in kit form.

**A weekly baking day was a tradition observed by many in the 1930s. Cakes and scones were on the menu when afternoon tea was a recognized meal, and lunch included a flan or pie as dessert.**

The fitted kitchen had not yet been invented. Most kitchens were furnished with a kitchen cabinet based on the bureau style: a closed cupboard at the bottom, glass-fronted at the top so that china (usually with a decorative floral pattern) could be seen, and with a pull-down flap at table height to provide an extra work surface on which plates could be laid out.

In addition there might be a small rectangular table with two fold-down flaps to save space when not in use. On the floor, quarry tiles or linoleum could be washed easily. Kitchens were often tiled to half-way up the wall, as this was thought hygienic.

Refrigerators were not common and in a real house, a larder leading off the kitchen would be used for most food storage. In the dolls' house, this could be simplified by storing food on shelves in the kitchen itself.

# Living rooms

The name for the room where the family would sit and relax has changed over the centuries. The solar, the withdrawing room, the parlour, the drawing room, the lounge and the sitting room all mean much the same thing, but there are definite distinctions of style, depending on what degree of formality or informality was expected at the time.

## Tudor or Jacobean hall and solar

The Tudor house was dominated by the hall, a large room which everyone also shared for eating and sleeping. The centrepiece was usually an oak refectory table with benches on either side and a chair at the head. The walls might be hung with tapestries or decorated with stencilling (*see* page 68), and a log fire in

An effective way of displaying a small collection of wind instruments is to attach them to the wall, using Blu-Tack. Be careful when fixing: it is all too easy to snap a slender wooden recorder in half by pressure applied at the wrong point.

Plain white walls are the perfect background for blackened beams. The fireplaces in this Tudor house are of cast resin which needs no painting to resemble stone. A log basket is essential.

the large fireplace would make the room look inviting.

The solar was a private room where the master of the house and his family could retreat from the hustle and bustle of a large household. Furniture was sparse but could include several rectangular wooden stools (known as 'joint stools' because of the method of construction) which were sometimes decorated with carving, and a wooden armchair for the master of the house. This too would have carved decoration, particularly on the back. An oak side table could hold pewter mugs and a flagon, or wooden plates or bowls.

Floors were uncovered, but a prized carpet was sometimes used as a table covering to add a rich effect. Carpets were far too valuable to walk on. The lady of the house would probably have an embroidery frame to work on (*see* picture). Music was a popular home entertainment and the Tudor solar can be brought to life by including some instruments.

## Queen Anne sitting room or parlour

During the reign of Queen Anne (1702–14) furniture styles changed to become more comfortable. The winged armchair was designed to protect its occupant from draughts and is still popular today. Panelled rooms were still much in use, with white-painted or walnut panelling. Lighting could come from girandoles (wall lights) – candle brackets backed by small mirrors to reflect the light.

A cosy Queen Anne parlour, complete with winged armchair and fine wooden furniture.

# Georgian drawing room

As the eighteenth century progressed manners became more formal. The family probably retreated to a small parlour in their leisure moments, but their drawing room, used for entertaining guests, tended to be severe and elegant. This is the ideal room to display a collection of fine miniatures, but bear in mind that the formality of the time extended to the arrangement of the furniture. Chairs were placed at intervals around the walls, and a dado rail was usually added to stop the chair backs from marking the paint or wallpaper (*see* page 64).

**Symmetry was much admired and ornaments were displayed in pairs if possible. Pictures were hung higher than would be customary today. A pole firescreen was obligatory, as it could be moved easily to protect the complexions of those sitting near the fire.**

# Regency drawing room

Life during the English Regency period (1811–20) was fairly boisterous and it became customary to arrange the seating in an informal manner, unlike the severity of the previous decades. Little tables were set ready to play cards and to hold drinking glasses, and comfortable sofas were placed near the fire. Decorations in the grander houses were ostentatious and this is one period where you can add gilded cornices and elaborate ornaments without overdoing things. A drawing room in such a house would also be bedecked with mirrors and candelabra.

**Compare this Regency drawing room with the more formal Georgian version shown on the left. A tea kettle is provided on a small table, ready for the hostess to dispense this new luxury during the evening. A young lady would be called upon to entertain the company by playing the square piano.**

# Victorian parlour

Early Victorian style was a simpler version of Regency elegance, but later in the nineteenth century, clutter abounded. For a dolls' house, a Victorian parlour of the period around 1880 can be great fun to put together. The more ornaments there are, the better, with rows of pictures in gilded frames hung on the walls (*see* page 96 for details on framing). Workboxes and footstools can be scattered about. Windows can be adorned with velvet or silk curtains edged with braid or bobble fringe, plus inner curtains of net or lace. For variety, blinds could be used in some rooms (*see* page 81 for instructions on making blinds).

Carpets add an air of comfort. These can be of needlepoint or cross stitch, and you can make them yourself, either from one of the many small-scale kits or charts which are available, or you can adapt a pattern from a full-size design if you have something specific in mind (*see* pages 81–2). Fitted carpets were becoming popular at this time, and one idea pioneered by Queen Victoria was to use plaid carpet. This is easy to reproduce using tartan woollen dress material, and can look very effective. The best way to lay fitted carpet is

Edwardian style is evoked by these small room settings, like the scullery shown on page 17, arranged in the deep front space of the Edwardian house. Care and thought has been given to the selection of a few items which bring the whole period to life.

A perfect finish is guaranteed with this comfortable-looking sofa and armchair made from a kit. It is supplied with a choice of small-patterned fabrics and comprehensive instructions which can be followed by absolute beginners.

matching armchairs, usually supplied with a choice of materials in suitable patterns. If your seams are not perfect, there is no need to worry: simply cover them with thin braid which can be glued or sewn on. A round table covered with a floor-length cloth could hold ornaments and photographs in silver frames. Vases of flowers will add to the fresh and luxurious look of the room.

# Dining room

The eating room, as it used to be called, has altered little in its basic arrangements over the years: it is merely the decorations that change.

with double-sided tape so that you can take it up easily when you feel it is time for a change.

# Rooms for modern living

For an up-to-date sitting room you might like to go for the 'country house' style that has been popular with professional interior decorators for the past decade. Be lavish with fabric (which is inexpensive for miniature settings) for curtains and cushions – use dress material with small prints, or Indian silks which are thin enough to hang well. Cover sofas and armchairs with floral print fabric. The trick when making a dolls' house cushion is to be economical with the stuffing. A small twist of acrylic wadding will be sufficient, as you want the cushion to look squashy and comfortable.

To furnish the room, easy chairs without arms are simple to make from scratch (*see* pages 88–9), or kits are available for a sofa and

This exquisitely painted service is laid on a table from a set of children's dolls' house furniture, demonstrating once again that it is possible to mix craftsman-made miniatures with very ordinary ones to good effect. The pears are glass beads.

Whatever the period, you will need a dining table and chairs (or benches) and some sort of sideboard – a plain oak trestle table for a Tudor room, or a bow-fronted mahogany sideboard for a Georgian room. A Georgian dining room should have a mahogany table, which can be set with a miniature dinner service, including glasses and perhaps a centrepiece of fruit in a glass or silver container. In a Victorian dining room a round dining table can be covered with a floor-length cloth (*see* pages 90–1).

The most important thing in a dining room is, of course, the food and a dolls' house dining table laid with a meal ready to eat always looks enticing. Professional miniaturists make delicious-looking models of a wide variety of food, but you can also make your own at little cost, using a modelling compound. Such compounds are now available in many colours and are simply hardened in the oven to make permanent. Follow the instructions given with the product and you will be surprised how easy it is. Be patient, and after a little practice you will be able to make food fit for a banquet. If you enjoy painting and are happy to spend a bit more time, it is more economical to use natural-coloured modelling compound and paint the pieces yourself.

# Bedroom

Throughout history the bedroom always seems to have been considered the woman's domain. Even if the rest of your dolls' house is quite plain, you might indulge in a spot of luxury for

This bed was copied from a similar version in an early Heal's catalogue. The comfortable-looking sprung mattress was specially made to fit the bed.

A white-painted metal bedstead with brass knobs would look well in an Edwardian bedroom: the lacy coverlet and satin eiderdown are typical of the time. The needlepoint rug was worked from one half of a design intended as a needlecase.

Hand-made patchwork quilts are always admired. These beautiful designs are (from left to right): 'Fence Posts', 'Sprigs and Roses', 'Grandma's Flower Garden' and 'Small Peaches'. For the novice, kits which include instructions, template, fine needles and pins, are available.

the main bedroom. Pretty floral prints, a draped dressing table (*see* page 91), curtains with tie-backs (*see* page 81) and a lace or patchwork bedspread all look delightful in miniature.

A bed is the easiest piece of furniture to make yourself using a small box as a base, which will be covered by the bedding. There is also a wonderful choice of ready-made 'antique' beds, some of which can be very pricey, depending on the craftsmanship involved. You may like to start off with a home-made bed while you save up for a real showpiece.

Keep in mind the size of the bedroom, however, because while a double bed or a four-poster may be impressive, it will probably take up too much of the available space in a small room (*see* page 4 for a size guide). It is sometimes wiser to choose a single bed for a modern room setting, or a half-tester rather than a four-poster.

Below left **A variety of bathroom accessories.**

# Bathroom

Bathrooms really only became standard features in houses in the 1930s. Until then it was usual to have a jug and basin on a marble-topped washstand in the bedroom. If your house is more modern, then a bathroom can look splendid, whether it is clean white or something rather more elaborate. Brass taps and 'glass' shelves (made of Perspex) will add sparkle and it is now possible to find 1/12-scale versions of everything from toothbrushes to soap at modest cost.

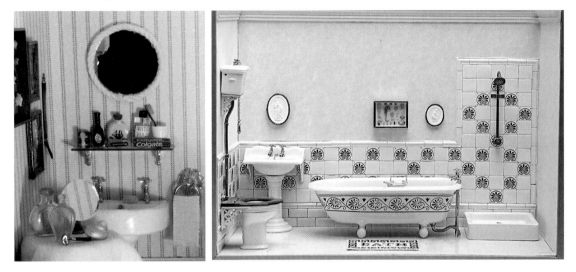

Above right **Black-and-white tiles and bath incorporating the Green Palmette pattern are effective in this striking bathroom which includes an early type of shower and a high-level cistern. Decorative plaster plaques and brass taps complete the setting.**

Left **A lavish Victorian country-house bathroom. The claw-foot bath has marbled sides. The water closet is a copy of Thomas Twyford's invention of 1883, the Unitas. A pine dressing-table and towel rail reinforce the period detail.**

I divided the ground floor of my early Victorian house to devote a large area to an impressive hall, an unusual feature in a dolls' house. In this period the usual place for the drawing room was the floor above, and a reception hall is appropriate. Given this amount of space, I was able to arrange a reception area for guests, and although in general I do prefer my houses unpopulated, the hall is usually a scene of bustling activity which includes both adult and child dolls.

A variety of garden ornaments enliven this hall. The urn, lion mask and acorn are painted to resemble verdigris (*see* pages 69–70). The attractive pendant light is a fake jewel, set in gold, from an old watch chain, and is suspended from a plaster ceiling rose.

# Entrance hall

Make the most of the entrance hall, whatever size it is. It is amazing what you can do with a space only about 3 by 5in (7.6 by 12.7cm), and if you have a large square hall, it can look magnificent. Even if it is tiny, however, the entrance sets the tone of the house so it is worth taking some trouble over it. In a Victorian house you might fit in an umbrella stand; in an Edwardian house there could be a hall stand for hanging hats and coats. Hang a picture or mirror on the wall; put a doormat or rug on the floor, and you instantly achieve a lived-in feel.

If you have a front porch this could be tiled. Use reproduction Victorian or Art Nouveau tiles, or black and white tiles in a chequerboard pattern. You can either fit real ceramic tiles or pieces of plasticized card. The card is thinner and, unlike the ceramic tiles, will not usually cause problems with opening the front door (*see* page 78 for how to adjust the front door if necessary).

# Unusual rooms

The rooms mentioned so far would all be found in the average home, but it is always an interesting challenge for the miniaturist to create a room setting which is out of the ordinary. If your house is large enough, or you are planning another dolls' house, or even if you are keen to include an unusual room in a small house, you might enjoy one of the ideas that follow.

# Nursery

Planning a nursery is fun and exciting in real life, and in a dolls' house can give continued enjoyment. My Victorian nursery contains far more toys than would be provided in reality and has developed over many years. The Victorian period is particularly rich in fascinating toys. Some of the 1/12-scale models are so tiny that they have to be made in metal for precision and durability. They also have moving parts and can be played with just like their full-size counterparts. Such items are a delight to seek out and collect, and are likely to catch the eye of any visitor.

**Whether Victorian or modern, a nursery can be one of the most interesting rooms to arrange. The toys in this one have been collected over many years.**

You might also consider including child dolls in a nursery. Even if you have no visible inhabitants in the rest of the house, dolls in the nursery make the whole scene come to life, especially if you have a rocking horse to set in motion.

# Dairy

I was first inspired to create a miniature dairy after admiring well-preserved examples of eighteenth- and nineteenth-century dairies at English stately homes open to the public.

**Blue and white 'tiled' wallpaper and decorative wall panels provide the appropriate background for this dairy. The wooden butter churn is a working model: the handle can be turned.**

Uppark and Lanhydrock both have evocative examples of a way of life long gone. I was entranced by the cool, functional interiors of the dairies and the range of pottery utensils neatly laid out. While this room setting would look out of place in a small house, it could certainly add an extra dimension to a farmhouse or country mansion.

# Eighteenth-century print room

Print rooms became popular in Regency times, and were often created by the ladies of the household, who would cut and paste up original prints to decorate the walls. The pictures were lithographs, usually of views, classical subjects or portraits of eminent people. A few print rooms still exist. I was so impressed with the arrangement at Stratfield Saye House (former country home of the great Duke of Wellington) that I decided to try some cutting and pasting myself.

I used a miniaturized sheet of print room designs to decorate the card room shown in the picture overleaf. An alternative would be to use prints cut from magazines and it is well worth keeping an eye out for suitable articles.

It is not necessary to fill all the walls of the room, which might be a little oppressive, especially on a small scale. For maximum effect, simply make an arrangement over the

Walls decorated with prints in the eighteenth-century fashion make the perfect setting for this Regency card room. Packs of miniature playing cards are inexpensive but difficult to keep tidy. I used only a few cards from a pack and arranged them as though in play, secured with dabs of Blu-Tack. The George III-style round table was used for many games with counters as well as cards. The lyre-end sofa table in the corner of the room would be needed for writing IOUs.

fireplace, round a door, or in a group over a side table. A border design on its own can also be effective. Even if you have no room to dedicate as a print room, you could consider the possibility of displaying prints in the hall and up the stairwell.

# Mackintosh room

The work of Charles Rennie Mackintosh (1868–1928) has become more widely known and appreciated in the second half of this century. In his own lifetime his designs astonished rather than impressed and were more valued by the avant-garde in Europe than in his native Scotland. A few years ago, I visited Glasgow and was able to see some of Charles Rennie Mackintosh's creations for myself. I became an instant admirer of his work. His hallmark of a strong, dark colour set against white can create a dramatic impression in miniature as well as in a full-size room.

If your dolls' house is of an appropriate period, this is a style well worth trying out in one room. I created a small room to show off

This room is a homage to Mackintosh style. The background colour is part of a set of cards from an exhibition of his work. The wall plaque is a copy of one by Margaret Mackintosh, who worked with her husband to create stylish rooms which were years ahead of their time.

a few treasured miniatures in Mackintosh style, and the effect was as startling and attractive as I had hoped.

# Loft conversions

A loft conversion is an excellent way of creating extra living space within an existing house. Some dolls' houses are also suitable for this treatment, and if you have sufficient space under the roof, you have the potential for

**Lift-off roof and attic space.**

**The furnished attic.**

creating a delightful and unusual setting, given the odd shape of the room with its sloping walls. There are several options for the attic conversion, depending on the structure of your dolls' house, and the examples given below may offer some practical ideas.

If you are unable to resist adding some 1/24-scale furniture and accessories to your collection of mainly 1/12-scale miniatures, then a loft space is the perfect place to arrange them, separated from the main house where they would be inappropriate.

The lift-off roof on the house shown opposite reveals a floor space 26in long by 8½in deep (66 by 21.5cm) and the only thing needed to convert it into a perfect working space for an artist or designer was to fit a planked floor (*see* page 78). Given the slope of the walls when the roof is in position, only the central portion of the floor can be used for furnishings, so careful positioning of any tall furniture is always necessary.

Some dolls' houses have hinged roofs, and the simpler ones may not even have a floor for the loft. This can easily be added, and the resulting floor space can be divided into two rooms with a triangular piece of wood, adding further flexibility to the new space created. Adding a non-opening door at the back will convey the impression of a staircase, or of other rooms behind (*see* picture page 55).

**The removable roof panel in my Wealden house.**

Another option is a removable panel in the roof, which lifts off to reveal a small loft space, as in the picture shown above. You can leave the loft room looking quite rough and ready, or smarten it up to the standard of the rooms below. For this house a planked floor was fitted and the square opening for the stair-ladder finished with thin stripwood. Stripwood was also added, varnished to match the exterior half-timbering on the house, to make a feature of the interior gable ends. The roof beams are ⅜in (10mm) square dowelling (*see* page 79 for advice on adding half-timbering).

# 4 *Shops*

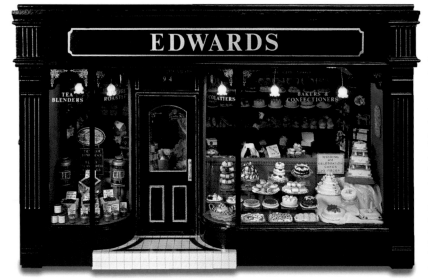

The sales floor and window displays are based on a tea-room in Harrogate, England, which has remained virtually unchanged since it opened in 1919. The miniaturist's own family grocery business traded for more than one hundred years, and he has an eye for a good display. The cakes are mouth-watering and you can almost smell the fragrances of the speciality teas and coffees.

A dolls' house shop can be an entertaining alternative to a miniature home as it can be adapted easily to a specific interest. Dolls' house shops are no more expensive than houses, and prices vary according to size and detailing in the same way. An antique shop, for example, can include furnishings and household goods of many different periods; a specialist shop could be ideal for the collector of miniature ceramics or woodturned objects which can be displayed on shelves and tables.

A shop is also the perfect way to show off your own handiwork if you enjoy a particular craft, be it miniature needlepoint carpets and cushions, pictures, or samplers. Your shop can stock anything you choose, depending on the space available – even a room box could be used. The following pages include a number of ideas for shops using a wide range of miniatures. For practical tips on fitting out your shop, see pages 103–4.

## Antique shop

An antique shop can hold a vast range of objects: again your only limit is the space available. If you occasionally buy furniture or ornaments on impulse to keep for some future project, they can all be kept in the shop for safe storage as well as for display, although you may never get round to moving them to their intended home. The shop can be full of

Above **Shelves fitted across the entire back wall of the shop provide useful storage for an assortment of decorative 'antiques'.**
Below **An old-fashioned perambulator can form part of the stock in an antique shop and is also useful for displaying dolls or, as in this case, teddy bears.**

expensive-looking fine furniture, or it could be more like a junk shop, according to your taste and the budget you have fixed.

You will probably want to include some display shelves, and these are simple to make (*see* page 85). A top hat, parasol and perhaps a pretty shawl might be displayed over an antique chair. Books can be neatly arranged on shelves or left in piles on the floor to add a suitably musty feel. You can make a whole collection of non-opening books inexpensively from a packet of coloured printed covers, available from dolls' house shops and suppliers. These simply need cutting out carefully and gluing round a small block of balsawood.

# Greengrocer or baker

Here are two 'foodie' ideas, both based on the kind of dolls' house shop which can be assembled from a kit. It is amazing how different the same basic structure can look with a change of decoration. To put together a well-stocked shop you could try your hand at making and painting miniature foodstuffs from modelling compound (*see* page 22), or you can buy an enormous range of delicious-looking foods from miniatures manufacturers.

Display cases and shelves are most often provided with the shop. Additional shelves can be bought separately, or made at home.

**Well-stocked bakery and grocery shops can be enormous fun to put together.**

# Art gallery

If one of your enthusiasms is for collecting or even painting miniature works of art, why not create an art gallery? There will be far more space to display your treasures than in a dolls' house full of furniture. Pictures look best hung in groups, and very superior ones can be displayed individually on easels. Ready-made miniature frames are easy to obtain, or you can take on the task of framing the pictures yourself (*see* page 96 for instructions).

design magazines and trendy shops in London and Bath, the contents of my shop will eventually be a miniature time capsule of 1990s decorative themes.

Depending on what takes your fancy, you could stock such a shop with bales of material, cushions, rugs, rolls of wallpaper, ornaments or small items of furniture. These are only suggestions: you can go down whatever route appeals to you.

My two-storey Georgian shop offers opportunities to arrange imaginative displays and has living accommodation 'over the shop' if required.

The exterior of the art gallery. A beautifully painted facade and some architectural additions transform a plain shop into a work of art in itself.

# Interior design shop

When I began writing this book, I had just acquired my latest dolls' house, based on an eighteenth-century shop. I have decorated the facade in typical Georgian style and colours, but decided the shop should be a modern interior design and decoration store. This allowed me to fill it with an assortment of frivolous and pretty objects, both bought and home-made. Inspired by ideas in interior

Inside the decorator shop. The stock is laid out to look as elegant as possible and so appeal to the customer who might patronize such a fashion-conscious establishment. Colour schemes in each room have been chosen to give a co-ordinated effect when the shop is open to view.

# 5 *Garden settings*

**The perfect miniature garden.**

Dolls' houses can be extended with the addition of a garden, and miniature gardening has distinct advantages over the real thing. You need not go out in the cold and get wet and muddy, but can garden in comfort on the dullest day. Climate and soil quality do not matter either.

If this is your first attempt at creating a dolls' house garden, you can start off with a simple design and then develop it into something more ambitious later on. If possible, allow extra space for 'growth' right from the start.

## Siting

The first point to consider is where to site the garden. A few dolls' house makers provide houses with a pull-out drawer for a garden at the base of the house, which can be stored away easily. Naturally, however, this adds to the cost and is really only suitable for a grand house.

Lacking such a useful accessory, I decided to create a garden room *inside* my Wealden house (*see* picture overleaf), where it reminds me of courtyard gardens glimpsed down passages or through entrance gates of similar sixteenth-century houses.

**A neat patio outside the front door gives a 'fresh-air' feel, even if there is no space for a proper garden.**

**Flagstones are essential for an effective garden courtyard. Plaster or cast resin wall plaques add to the out-of-doors feeling. Plants in pots and tubs or on a pedestal can be moved around to suit your mood or the season, making a changing scene which will give lasting pleasure.**

Miniature garden pots in jewel-like colours will add interest to even the tiniest patio. Here arranged on gravel, the pots have been planted with long-lasting miniature cacti.

For the smaller house, an ideal place for a tiny garden or patio is at the side of the house. All you need to do is add a base board of a size to suit your ideas. It is best to use a piece of sturdy blockboard about ⅝in (16mm) thick. Blockboard or MDF are available from timber merchants or home decoration stores. If you plan to attach a lean-to conservatory to the house, the base board will need to be secured firmly. Use two large hinges or, if available, strips of metal drilled for screws, and fix these to the base of the house and the base of the blockboard, where they will not show. If you do not plan to attach anything more than creeper to the house, the board can be left separate and merely butted against the house wall.

# Planning

However small your garden or patio, the secret of success is good planning. Design it on paper first, making sure that you can fit all the features you want into the space available. If you have a period-style house you can design a garden which will complement it perfectly. The 'Practical Gardening' section on pages 105–8 will give you all the details you need for creating the garden you want, but here are a few suggestions to set the ball rolling.

# Ideas for period-style gardens

## Tudor or Jacobean herb garden

Design a knot garden, with beds of flowers and herbs arranged in a formal pattern. Arrange earth or paved paths between beds.

## Georgian formal garden

Square or rectangular beds of flowers can be divided up by gravel paths. Neatly trimmed low hedges should surround the flower beds, with small standard trees placed at regular intervals.

A wedding-cake pillar gives height to this arrangement of exquisite flowers.

## Victorian flower garden

A piece of sculpture makes a good centrepiece, and you can use a wedding-cake pillar as a pediment for a statue or urn. Surround with plenty of colourful flowers, paved or grassed in between the beds.

## Cottage garden

A winding path can be created from miniature bricks or paving made from modelling compound, with fake moss glued into the cracks. A miniature stone sink makes a good container for fake or dried plants and flowering creeper.

# Garden buildings

A garden building will make an attractive addition to your miniature garden or patio. This need not be expensive. You can adapt something yourself (*see* page 107) to make a greenhouse at very little cost, but if you are keen to add on a very superior conservatory, be prepared to pay out rather more. There are some very grand models available, which, if you do not mind the expense, can add a spectacular extra dimension to your dolls' house.

A garden shed or rabbit hutch will add charm to an informal garden (*see* picture below). Home-made buildings can be effective, especially if you want to achieve a more homely or rough-hewn look.

# Garden accessories

It is always fun to give the impression that some activity has been going on in the dolls' house garden to add life to the scene. A watering can and a mini-trowel or garden fork can be left ready for use, together with a few plant pots and some packets of seeds. Seed packets can be made simply by folding small pieces of paper into envelopes and writing the plant name clearly using a fine-line pen. A coiled green shoelace with a metal end will make an effective garden hose.

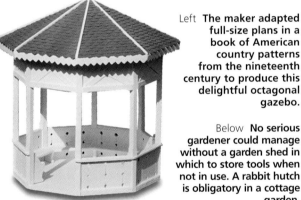

Left **The maker adapted full-size plans in a book of American country patterns from the nineteenth century to produce this delightful octagonal gazebo.**

Below **No serious gardener could manage without a garden shed in which to store tools when not in use. A rabbit hutch is obligatory in a cottage garden.**

**A miniature wheelbarrow and other tools can bring a garden scene to life.**

# Upkeep

A miniature garden does need a certain amount of maintenance – to keep dust rather than weeds at bay. Go over it occasionally with a small feather to flick off dust, and if necessary use a moist cotton bud and a small piece of damp cloth. If you include dried flowers rather than plastic ones you will need to replace them occasionally to keep the garden looking fresh and colourful. There is nothing worse than deadlooking plants.

# 6 *Dolls' houses for children*

Providing a house for a child is a delightful introduction to the world of dolls' houses. There are few constraints on period: you can imagine and create anything you like which will please the new home owner. There are important points to consider, however, as the house will be treated as a plaything by the child, rather than as a showcase by the adult miniatures collector.

## Houses for different ages

### Under-fives

Dolls' houses stocked by toy shops (as opposed to specialist dolls' house shops) and available by mail order from toy manufac-turers, are specifically designed for young children. It is vital that a dolls' house intended for play should be sturdy and not easily damaged. If the child is younger than five, try to find one which is open plan and accessible from both back and front, so that it can be played with by two or three children together. This type of house is usually sold flat-packed, and tends to be relatively inexpensive. The usual scale is 1/12, although houses for very young children may be larger.

## Five- to eight-year-olds

For children aged five years and upwards, a house with a prettily decorated front will be

This house, aptly named Blossom Cottage, is ideal for five- to eight-year-olds. The kit is made from MDF and simply clicks together without the need for glue or screws. One room per floor without divisions allows easy access so that two children can play together.

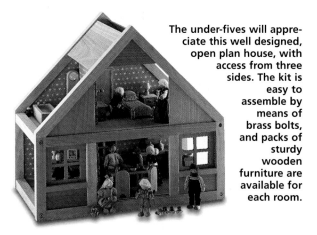

The under-fives will appreciate this well designed, open plan house, with access from three sides. The kit is easy to assemble by means of brass bolts, and packs of sturdy wooden furniture are available for each room.

popular. The exteriors of some simple kit houses are screen-printed to resemble a cottage-style house, complete with roses round the door, and there is no need for additional painting. Again, any fixtures and fittings need to be sturdy, but some more delicate items can be added as the children become more dextrous and interested in detail.

## Nine years and over

For the older child of nine years or more, it is worth investing in a proper, 1/12-scale house. If the child becomes interested in the dolls' house as an ongoing hobby, inexpensive first furniture can be replaced gradually with more 'collectable' items in the internationally accepted scale.

This house was planned by an architect and its simplified Georgian facade makes it equally suitable for child or collector. It is available either ready built and painted, or in kit form, and the windows have screenprinted glazing bars. Behind the pediment, a flat roof provides sufficient space to add an optional roof garden or terrace.

## Decoration and fittings

Even if the house is intended as a Christmas or birthday surprise, it is probably better not to decorate it completely. Why not let the child become involved right from the start? He or she will enjoy the house much more if allowed

to contribute, and a large part of the pleasure of owning a dolls' house is to fit out the inside. It is not beyond the capabilities of most average eight-year-olds to help make curtains, fit carpets or even paper walls, with a little help and guidance.

It is best not to use expensive mouldings to start with, as a child will not appreciate beautifully mitred joins. Instead, use plain stripwood from a model shop, which is much cheaper, and butt this together at the corners to provide simple skirting boards. Use general purpose glue rather than permanent wood glue, so that these mouldings can be removed later on and replaced with better quality materials, when the child is ready to enjoy the detail.

## Furniture

Some commercially made dolls' house furniture sold in toy shops and department stores today is in 1/16 scale. This is a legacy from the old Triang dolls' houses (*see* pages 110–11) and later a make called Caroline's

A cradle made from a walnut shell, or, as shown here, a small wooden box, will give great pleasure, especially if it contains a tiny baby doll. The doll can be a small bead, marked out to resemble a face, attached to a basic cloth body and wrapped in scraps of lace trimmings. A set of bowls are simply acorn cups painted gold, while the tiny rabbits may be preferred to dolls by a small child who is fond of animals.

Home, which some readers may remember from the 1960s. In general, young children are not much worried by inconsistencies of scale (although older children may find it very important as they often like to have everything just so). A mixture of such ready-made furniture with home-made items and some plain, strong wooden furniture, which can be painted or stencilled by the child, will be ideal for a first dolls' house. Nothing needs to be expensive, so that it will not be a tragedy when breakages occur.

# Simple decoration ideas

The decorative theme for a child's dolls' house may stem from a small toy the child already owns, a favourite story, or something which he or she likes collecting. The following are some ideas from my own experience.

## A Tudor house

Half-timbered houses always seem to appeal to children (as they do to many adults), and it is possible to obtain inexpensive and hard-wearing models with the beams screen-printed on the facade. Inside you can decorate by hanging paper 'tapestries' on the wall, cut from magazine advertisements. An old lid from a small jar can be used to hold pot pourri (regular pot pourri shredded smaller). A plastic chandelier is cheap but adds an impressive touch.

**This East Anglian style half-timbered house is unusual for a British-made house in that access is from the rear opening. Supplied fully-finished, it is fitted with 'leaded' windows, inglenook fireplaces and a staircase. A less expensive timber-framed cottage is also available.**

# A sea captain's house

Interest in dolls' houses is certainly not confined to small girls. Boys are often fascinated by anything miniature, especially if this includes items with miniscule moving parts. They may enjoy playing with a dolls' house just as much as the girls. A dolls' house for a boy can be based on any theme of special interest, or a current hobby, whether it is sport or collecting.

**The sea captain's house, complete with lobster pot and a chart to show the location of buried treasure.**

My little grandsons are thrilled with their dolls' house, a home for a retired sea captain. It is filled with fishy miniatures, nautical objects and even a tiny ship in a bottle. The sea captain has a parrot and a miniature shell collection, and is surrounded by souvenirs from his voyages in the China Seas. The house has inspired all sorts of inventive games and has led to an ever-increasing shell collection which now extends out of the house to include larger specimens too.

## Other decorative ideas

No decorative features in a child's dolls' house need be expensive. A satisfactory effect can be achieved very easily with the most mundane of materials.

■ Furnishing braid makes good stair carpet: fixed with double-sided tape, it is easily replaced during redecoration.

- An open staircase can be made 'safe' with a side panel of plain needlepoint canvas, brushed with all-purpose glue to make it stiffer, then painted white.
- An elaborate plasterwork ceiling can be made out of a simple paper doyley. Give the ceiling a base coat of emulsion first, and when that is dry, carefully glue on the doyley, cut to fit. Apply a second coat of emulsion, working gently so that the doyley does not tear.
- Walls and mantelpieces can be adorned with tiny pictures cut from magazines and glued on to jewellery 'frames'.
- Use old clip earrings to hold back curtains or bed canopies.

# Dolls' house dolls or toys

'People' are essential for a child's dolls' house. They need not be dolls: very young children might prefer small, furry animals, miniature mice, or teddy bears.

**A group of wooden-headed dolls, all dressed for a wedding.**

An older child will probably want a family of dolls. Peg dolls are inexpensive and easy to make from old-fashioned, wooden clothes pegs, but the disadvantage with the standard peg doll is that it cannot be made to sit down. Watching my grandchildren playing with their dolls' houses, I realize how important such things are. If they want to arrange a tea party, or sit the doll on a chair, then a stiff, stand-up doll simply will not do. It is not difficult to make sit-down peg dolls, and instructions are given on page 92. These can be dressed in any way you wish.

# Christmas in the dolls' house

Children invariably become excited around Christmas time, and most love being involved in preparations, decorations and the general hustle and bustle. Why not extend Christmas to the dolls' house? If the children have a dolls' house of their own, they can have enormous fun decking it out with miniature decorations, which they can make themselves, with a bit of help. If you also own an 'adult' collector's dolls' house, and you have time to spare, you

**Christmas festivities and decorations can be enjoyed to the full in the miniature scale.**

could decorate that too, perhaps at the last minute as a surprise for the children on Christmas Day. Some suggestions for miniature Christmas decorations follow:

- Fix a wreath on the front door.
- Provide a miniature Christmas tree: a section from a bottle brush works well when dyed green and sprinkled with glitter.
- Make a pile of parcels from assorted small blocks of wood or boxes, wrapped in coloured shiny paper.
- Crochet a 'paper-chain' from gilt parcel string, or two strands of red or green embroidery cotton.
- Make Christmas cards by cutting out small details from used cards. Some Christmas

catalogues have mini-reproductions of cards which can be used as they are.
- Cut out small stockings from felt (one thickness only) and hang near the fireplace.
- Make special festive food from modelling compound.

**These Christmas decorations and food are all professionally made. Just like our full-size decorations, they are carefully packed away each year, ready for when Christmas comes round again.**

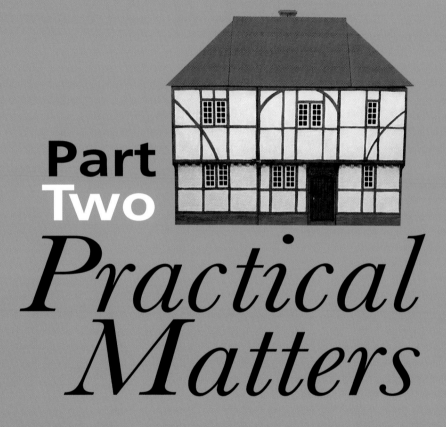

# Part Two

## Practical Matters

# 7 *Building a house from a kit*

Many newcomers to the dolls' house hobby will prefer to buy a ready-made house and concentrate on the decoration and furnishings. If you have decided to take on the challenge (and financial saving) of constructing your own house, however, here are some practical tips to supplement the instructions provided by the manufacturer.

1 Check first that all the parts are included in the kit. Lay them out and familiarize yourself with them.
2 Read carefully the instructions provided, check the parts mentioned in each stage of assembly and make sure that you understand how they fit together.
3 Sand each piece until smooth with fine glasspaper, grade 0 or 00.
4 Check that any pre-cut grooves are the right size to take slot-in parts. You may need to make minute adjustments by sanding to ensure a perfect fit.
5 Assemble each stage 'dry' and check that all is correct before you use wood glue. Once the glue has set it will be impossible to undo.
6 While the glue is setting, it is best to hold the pieces firmly together with masking tape, as it will take several hours until full strength is achieved.
7 It is essential to ensure that walls and floors are at right angles, or you could end up with a leaning house. Check every angle with a set square and, if you do not have an appropriately equipped workshop, improvise a jig by using blocks of wood with perfectly squared corners, or even piles of books, which I find work well. Use the jig to support the structure while the glue dries.
8 If a staircase is provided in the kit, but is not designed to be built in during the initial assembly, it is far more practical not to glue it in place until after you have decorated the rooms.

This Edwardian terrace house has all the charm of the period and can be built from a kit or supplied assembled. The basic kit is two storeys plus an attic room. A basement kit can be added to provide two extra rooms and a service entrance behind the railings and gate. The dormer window is another optional extra.

Once constructed, your kit house will be at the same stage as an undecorated, ready-made model: waiting for the first steps in the decorative process which will turn the shell of the house into something bright, expressive and personal.

**Victoria House is based on a typical Victorian house on the Isle of Anglesey. It is supplied ready-assembled, but for the woodworker all the parts can be supplied separately. There are six rooms and two back windows let in extra light.**

# 8 *Twenty steps to basic decoration*

You are bound to be impatient to start on the decoration of your new dolls' house, but it pays not to be in too much of a hurry. Care and thought at each stage will ensure good results. Before you begin decorating, it is important to prepare the surfaces and, unless the house is to be, in effect, no more than a series of boxes joined together, you will probably want to install some fixtures and fittings.

**This shop can be supplied assembled or to build from a kit. A shop with living accommodation above it provides plenty of scope for the hobbyist to arrange the interior in an individual way. This shell provided the basis for my interior design shop (*see* page 30).**

The following check list gives my 'twenty steps' of basic decoration, and sets out a logical order for the work. Detailed instructions for each process follow the initial list, together with step-by-step guides for making basic fixtures. The woodwork required for such additions is simple for the beginner, using the tools listed on pages 46–7. If you are really averse to tackling woodwork of any kind, however, there are ways of getting round this (*see* page 62). The simple paint finishes listed on page 44 will be effective for both exterior and interior. For the more ambitious, a variety of options for more elaborate decorative treatments are also detailed in Chapter 9.

---

### Lighting

You may want to consider the option of adding electric lighting to the house and it is best to make this decision right at the start. If you decide in favour of lighting, it is easier to arrange it *before* decorating so that wires can be concealed (*see* page 48).

---

## Twenty steps check list

**Preparation**
1  Smooth over both **exterior and interior surfaces** with fine glasspaper.
2  **Fill any cracks** with filler and leave to

This is the interior of the shop. My original intention was to use only the lower part as a shop and have a living room and bedroom above, but during the planning stage I changed my mind and decided to devote the entire building to display space.

dry. For this purpose, interior plaster filler is better than wood filler as it is finer. Sand again.

3  Make sure that the house is **free of dust** before you begin painting. If possible use a suction cleaner with a fine nozzle attachment.

4  **Paint** both exterior and interior walls with quick-drying primer or undercoat.

5  Apply two coats of emulsion to the **ceilings**. One coat is sufficient if you plan any special treatment later.

### Exterior decoration

6  Paint the **exterior walls** (*see* page 66) and the roof (*see* page 45).

7  Paint **window** and **door frames** (*see* page 45).

8  Paint the **front door**. Door furniture (knob, letterbox, knocker, etc.) can be fitted at this stage, or after the decorations are completed (*see* page 46).

### Interior design (stages in blue are optional)

9  Fit any **lighting** (*see* page 48).

10  Make and site **chimney breasts** (*see* pages 49–51).

11  Make **fireplaces** (*see* page 49).

12  Make any required additions to **staircase** (balusters, newel posts, side panel, *see* pages 53–4).

13  Fit **flooring** (*see* pages 55–6).

14  Fit **internal doors** (*see* pages 56–7).

### Interior decoration

15  **Paint walls** in your chosen colours (*see* page 58).

16  **Wallpaper walls** if required as an alternative to paint (*see* pages 59–61).

17  Add wallpaper **borders** (*see* pages 61–2).

### Fittings

18  Fit **door frames** (*see* page 62).

19  Cut, paint and fit **skirtings, cornice** and **dado rail** or **picture rail** (*see* pages 61–4).

20  Cut and fit **window glazing** and **internal window frames** if required (*see* page 65).

# Preparation

For the initial preparation and exterior decoration you will need the following:

- Glasspaper, grades 00 to 3
- Interior plaster filler
- Orange stick
- Emery board
- Good quality paintbrushes, sized ½in (13mm), ¾in (19mm) and 1in (25mm)
- Fine art paintbrushes for small details, sizes 00 to 3 and size 5

Although decorating a dolls' house is much less tiring than full-size decoration, it is certainly more fiddly and care is needed to achieve a perfect result. It is vital to prepare the surface well, because in such a small scale any tiny blemish or hairline crack will show up badly after decoration.

After sanding all surfaces with fine glasspaper, fill any cracks with interior plaster filler. An orange stick is the best thing to use for pushing filler right into the joints. When this has set, sand smooth and remove any loose dust.

---

### Sanding

Wrap glasspaper round a small block of wood to avoid rounding off corners. Do not go on using glasspaper which is worn, as it will be ineffective.

An emery board (the kind used for nail care) is perfect for smoothing the corners of window frames, door frames and glazing bars. It will go into tight corners and can also be used while you are painting: if you see a slight bump missed in the earlier sanding, rub down with the emery board and paint over it to produce a really smooth finish.

---

### Using filler

It is difficult to mix a small enough amount of filler for most dolls' house work. It is possible to keep the filler workable for a short time by gathering what is left into a lump and wrapping it closely in damp clingfilm.

If you prefer to use ready-mixed interior filler, be warned that this, too, dries up if exposed to air. Take out a small quantity from the carton and put it in an eggcup while working, resealing the carton.

---

Next, undercoat the exterior and interior walls, even if you plan to wallpaper certain rooms. This will prevent any marks or colour in the wood from showing through later. It is worth rubbing over the undercoat, when dry, with size 00 glasspaper.

Topcoat the ceilings with emulsion paint.

# Suitable paints for exterior and interior use

The list below is a guide to the best paints to use on different parts of your dolls' house.

| Type of paint | Where to use |
| --- | --- |
| Emulsion paint | Interior walls, ceilings and as undercoat on thin wood mouldings. Emulsion is available in sample pots, which are often a suitable size for dolls' house decoration. |
| Gloss paint | Do not use on a dolls' house, with the possible exception of the front door. The excessive shine looks unrealistic in small scale. |
| Semi-matt paint | Satin finish is best for exterior walls, door and window frames, roofs and interior paintwork. |
| Model paint | Useful on its own or as a mixer with emulsion to make more interesting colours for roofs, ornaments and accessories (see example page 69). Available from hobby shops. |
| Gouache | A small amount mixed with emulsion and diluted with a splash of water will produce glowing colours for walls and roofs (see pages 66–7) to simulate colour-washed cob or plaster. The mix will not be waterproof and must be finished with a coat of matt or semi-matt varnish. Available from suppliers of artists' materials. |
| Acrylic | Can be mixed to make realistic shades for roof tiles or slates (see page 73). Available from hobby shops or suppliers of artists' materials. |

# Exterior decoration

## Walls

Paint the exterior walls with two coats of satin finish semi-matt paint in the colour of your choice. Any architectural features can be added at a later stage (*see* pages 73–5). For special paint finishes and textured treatments, see pages 66–8.

The pale yellow paint used on the facade of this Regency house was a popular choice in the early nineteenth century. Alternatives might be apricot or a pale green. A bright bronze-green was usual for ironwork, but I chose white to emphasize the added roof ridging for a more frivolous effect.

## Roofs

Model paints can give an excellent finish on a plain roof. You will need the larger can for most roofs, as two coats will be necessary to give a good overall covering. A matt-finish medium grey will suit most dolls' houses.

If you have not done much painting, you might wish to try out a practice piece on a spare bit of wood first, to test out your skills in achieving a smooth finish.

## Window frames

When painting the glazing bars on fixed-in windows, it is easy to miss the underneath or one side of some of the bars. The best way to avoid this is to establish an order of work:

This exquisitely detailed window was made for a house based on Robert Adam's own home in London, long since demolished. Adam's original drawings still exist.

paint the underneath and one side of each section in sequence, then the other side and lastly the top of each. This will avoid the annoyance of coming back to admire your work later, only to find that some parts have been missed. (*See* page 65 for details of how to fit window glazing.)

## Front door

The choice of colour for a front door is very personal. For a Tudor or Jacobean house the choice will be made for you: the door should

The small porch and keystone detail above this six-panelled door are typical of many houses in the English Cotswolds. The door is stained as oak.

**White against a dark green facade makes a striking contrast on a bow-windowed eighteenth-century shop.**

be stained or varnished to resemble oak. The use of gloss paint should be restricted to a black front door for a Victorian town house, or a brightly coloured one for a child's dolls' house, otherwise semi-matt paint should be used.

White paint will accentuate any special details on a porch, and will make a feature of a pillared portico, especially if this is contrasted with a darker house wall.

## Door furniture

A doorknob is usually already fitted on a purchased dolls' house, or comes supplied with a kit house. You might add a lion's-head knocker to a country house door, or an Adam-style brass doorknocker to a Georgian or Regency one. Houses of later periods can also have a letter box. Carriage lamps may look good on either side of an imposing entrance. All these extras are available from dolls' house

stockists. Door knobs usually need to be screwed on, but door knockers, letter boxes and bell pushes can be glued on with all-purpose glue.

# Interior design

It is far simpler in the long run to decide on the design features you wish to include *before* you begin any interior decoration. Do you, for example, want to install any lighting? Does your house have chimneys, and if so, where will you site the fireplaces? What kind of flooring would you like in each room? Are you going to fit internal doors? All these features can be planned at an early stage.

## Tools

You will need the following basic tools to fit out the interior.

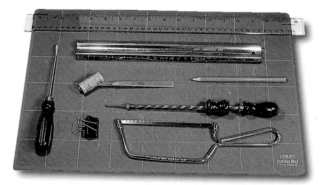

**These tools are essential if you plan to add fittings and fixtures to your dolls' house. *From the top:* plastic and metal rulers, craft knife, pencil, small screwdriver, bradawl, bulldog clip, gent's saw.**

- Small screwdrivers (of a size used for small electrical work)
- Bradawl (a pointed tool for starting a hole in wood to insert screws)
  Note: in soft wood, a thick darning needle used with a thimble to protect your thumb is often sufficient to start a hole.
- Craft knife
- Metal ruler with a raised edge for use as a cutting guide

■ Self-healing cutting mat marked out with a squared grid (available from art materials suppliers)
■ Metal mitre box and saw (e.g. X-Acto mitre box no. 7533 and knife handle no. 5 fitted with saw blade no. 239 – but other makes are available, all a fairly standard size, from suppliers of miniature tools)
■ Gent's saw, 7in (178mm) long
■ Pencils
■ Bulldog clips
■ Masking tape
■ Magnifier for checking fine detail

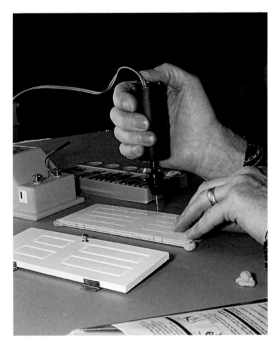

A miniature electric drill: this is not essential and is an expensive extra tool if you plan only one dolls' house, but for the committed hobbyist it makes fitting door knobs or hinges much easier.

## Sharp tools

Blades on craft knives must be changed frequently. They are inexpensive and are only effective when sharp. If you cut any acetate for window glazing, change the blade as soon as you have finished, as it will be blunted.

A good pair of scissors will be adequate for some purposes, but it is far more difficult to cut perfectly straight lines on paper or card. Using the grid on a cutting mat will save a great deal of time and trouble when cutting parallel edges on wallpaper, etc.

Sharpen pencils often: the width of the line made by a blunt pencil will make measurements inaccurate.

## Safety first

**Treat all cutting tools with respect.**

### Rule 1
Always check before you cut that your free hand is behind the blade and not in front of it, to avoid accidents.

### Rule 2
Never use cutting tools if you are tired, when it becomes too easy to make a mistake. There is always another day.

### Rule 3
Always put a craft knife down while you check or adjust the position of the work. It is easy to forget that you are holding it and to nick yourself.

# Adhesives

You will also need to use a variety of adhesives, depending on the task in hand. Modern adhesives are not interchangeable and work best on the materials for which they are intended. The check list of glues overleaf is a brief guide to what is suitable for different materials.

Tools and glues can be stored away neatly inside the dolls' house while work is in progress. An eggcup makes a useful container for tiny screws.

| Type of glue | Where to use |
|---|---|
| All-purpose clear adhesive | For card, paper, wood, ceramics (e.g. UHU and Bostik). |
| PVA white wood adhesive | For *permanent* fixing of wood: once set, the bond cannot be undone. Evo-Stik Resin 'W' is widely available. |
| Rubber-based adhesive | To attach ceramic tiles to card or wood. Do not use on fabric as this type of glue (e.g. Copydex) yellows with age. |
| Epoxy resin | This is an extra-strong, all-purpose glue mixed from two tubes before use. It will provide an exceptionally strong bond on small parts, e.g. metal feet attached to wooden legs on furniture. |
| Polystyrene cement | Useful for the dolls' house garden as it will not dissolve polystyrene (used to make fake rocks). |
| Paper glue | Limited use as it is easy to over-wet paper and leave a crinkled effect. Use on thick paper only. Useful for the dolls' house garden to fix flock powder in place. |
| Superglue | To attach ceiling roses, etc. Position with care. Wipe off fingers immediately before touching anything and before fixing part. |

### Glue fumes

Most glues produce fumes to some extent and it is essential to work in a well ventilated room, preferably with the window open. I have been in one dolls' house maker's workshop where the fumes were so strong that I found it difficult to breathe. The craftsman did not even notice the effect, probably due to repeated exposure. Glue fumes are definitely not good for you, whether you notice them or not, and exposure to concentrated amounts can be dangerous.

Electric lighting transforms this house into a lively and homely looking place.

# Lighting

If you wish to install electric lighting in your dolls' house, the easiest way to tackle it is to buy a kit (Cir-Kit, for example) which suits the number of rooms you have. Booklets are available by mail order and from dolls' house shops which will take you through every stage of the installation. Provided you follow the manufacturer's instructions, fitting the system is within the capabilities of a beginner.

Kits work from a 12-volt battery or a transformer. Copper tape wires can be fixed to the floors and concealed under the floor covering. It is also possible to obtain skirting boards with a groove at the back for the wires.

There will be some future expense in replacing batteries from time to time, if you do not have a transformer, and changing very small bulbs in a restricted space can be difficult unless you are dextrous. Should a fault occur in concealed wiring, you may also have to redecorate after you have located and repaired it. The effect of a beautifully lit dolls' house is magical, however, and as long as you are prepared to undertake occasional maintenance work, it will definitely be worth the effort involved.

# Chimney breasts and fireplaces

Fitting a chimney breast is not obligatory. It is perfectly feasible to fit a fireplace directly on to the wall and assume an exterior flue (*see* picture, page 50). This is often the best option in a small bedroom where the bed will take up much of the space. On the other hand, most sitting rooms, whatever the period of the house, will look more interesting if the fireplace is fitted to a chimney breast. This will also provide useful alcoves on either side for display shelves, small items of furniture, or pictures. If you do want a chimney breast in a small room, why not fit it in one corner to save space? Instructions for making standard and corner chimney breasts are given on pages 50–2.

**Elegant Adam-style fireplaces in cast resin need no painting. A simple marble hearth (*see* picture page 64) will complement this style perfectly. Fenders were not in general use in an eighteenth-century home.**

Before you make the chimney breast, however, in order to get the measurements right, you need to decide on the style and size of the fireplace. Fireplaces in various styles are available from dolls' house stockists, and are beautifully crafted. Some period rooms will look perfect with one of these elaborately 'carved' fireplaces made in cast resin or plaster. If you do not wish to buy ready-made, you can design and build your own fireplace from pieces of wood mouldings, and you can make it as plain or elaborate as you wish. Details for constructing a basic fireplace follow.

**I chose a deep cornice moulding for this simple fireplace. The height of the finished fireplace should relate to the height of the room. Check out a suitable size with a cardboard cut-out before you decide what will look best.**

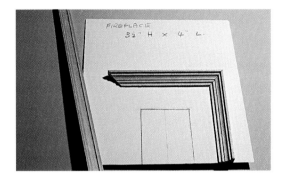

## Basic fireplace

### Materials

- Short lengths of wood mouldings
- Paint of your choice (semi-matt finish)
- Marbled paper or tiles for grate surround
- Stiff card

### Method

1. Decide on the size of your finished fireplace. Plan out on card.
2. Cut three pieces of wood moulding to the required lengths. Mitred joins are essential for a neat fit at the corners. Place the wood in the mitre block with the plain back surface horizontal. Cut from the outer to the inner edge of the join (*see* diagram below). Check that the two side pieces are exactly the same length.

**Cutting the mitred corners for a fireplace.**

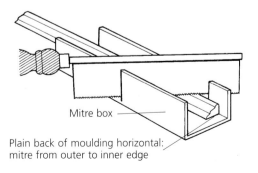

Mitre box

Plain back of moulding horizontal: mitre from outer to inner edge

3 Glue together with all-purpose adhesive.

4 Undercoat and topcoat with your chosen paint.

5 Cut the grate aperture on your card plan. Glue the tiles or marbled paper on to the card to form the grate surround, and finally glue on the fireplace itself.

If, like me, you enjoy experimenting and want to produce a fireplace with a grander look, the pictures below offer ideas for more elaborate fireplaces. There are any number of variations on the theme. Once you have made up the basic fireplace above, you will see how easy it would be to build up more complicated designs. The fireplaces in these pictures are still at the design stage and are roughly fixed with Blu-Tack to the chimney breast to judge the effect. Some of the stripwood has been undercoated to make the sequence of assembly clear.

**Trying out designs for more elaborate fireplaces can be great fun. The designs below are based on real examples; the one with the pink marble insert is especially flamboyant. The fireplace with a black marble surround (a new use for last year's desk diary cover) was planned to incorporate two fake Wedgwood plaques.**

In this case, the finished fireplace is fitted directly on to the wall without a chimney breast. I have added a plain mantelshelf of stripwood and filled in the open grate with a chimneyboard, which is simply a picture of one, mounted on card. The stone detailing above the fireplace is also paper, mounted on card, to give the impression that this is an older-style fireplace in a room which has been updated in Georgian times.

## Basic chimney breast

### Materials

- Balsawood, ½–¾in (13–19mm) thick (available from hobby shops)
  *or*
- Polyboard, a layer of foam sandwiched between two layers of card (available from art materials shops)
  Note: like balsawood, polyboard can be cut with a small saw or craft knife. Both materials crumble easily so need to be cut carefully.
- Thin, matt black card.

### Method

1 Measure the height of the room. The chimney breast should be the same height. Its width should be 1in (25mm) more than the *widest* part (usually the mantelshelf) of the planned fireplace, to allow approximately ½in (13mm) on either side.

**Putting together a basic chimney breast.**

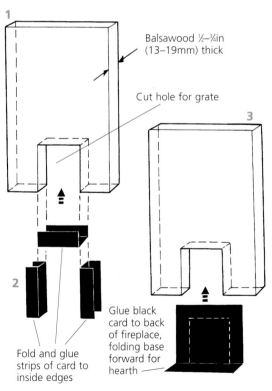

Balsawood ½–¾in (13–19mm) thick

Cut hole for grate

2

Fold and glue strips of card to inside edges

Glue black card to back of fireplace, folding base forward for hearth

2 Cut the balsawood or polyboard to the correct size.

3 Using the fireplace as a guide, mark and cut an opening for the grate in the chimney breast, making sure that it is central (*see* diagram 1).

4 The sides and top of the grate opening need to be black. Cut three small strips of matt black card about 1½in (38mm) wide, one measuring the same as the width of the opening and two the same as the height. Fold and glue over the sides and top of the grate opening (*see* diagram 2). The card edges will be concealed at the back, and at the front will be covered by the fireplace.

5 Cut another piece of the matt black card approximately 1in (25mm) deeper and wider than the opening. Glue this across the back of the chimney breast to cover the opening with an overlap of ½in (13mm) all round, to make a fireback. Fold the spare ½in (13mm) of card at the base forward, to make a floor for the grate (*see* diagram 3).

6 Double check that the grate openings on the chimney breast and fireplace are the same size. Glue the chimney breast in place, and decorate along with the rest of the room. The fireplace should be glued on last of all.

## Corner fireplace and chimney breast

A space-saving corner chimney breast can be made for a small room from a piece of good-quality cardboard. The card fits diagonally across the corner of the room, leaving a gap behind.

### Materials

- Firm cardboard
- Balsawood *or* polyboard
- Matt black card
- Prepared fireplace (small)
- Beading/stripwood (optional)

### Method

1 Measure the height of the room and the width of the angled space to be covered

(the width of the fireplace, plus ½in [13mm] either side). Cut the card the same height as the room and 3in (76mm) wider than the angled space.

2　Score the card 1½in (38mm) from each side edge and fold the two 'wings' back and inwards. These will be glued against the walls on either side (*see* diagram 1).

3　Cut a piece of balsawood or polyboard the same height as the chimney breast but 2in (51mm) narrower than the card. Glue this centrally to the back of the card to strengthen it (see diagram 1).

4　Cut an opening for the grate through both card and balsawood (or polyboard). Finish with black card as in steps 4 and 5 in the method for the basic chimney breast (*see* diagram 2).

5　Fix the chimney breast in place by gluing the side wings to the walls on either side. The join can be covered by a thin strip of beading. The fireplace should be added after everything else has been decorated.

**Creating a corner chimney breast.**

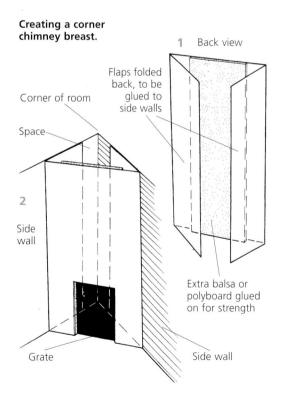

Planning a corner fireplace is a little more complicated: the fireplace should not be more than 3½in (89mm) wide, or it will take up too much floor space. The ends of the mantelshelf can fit neatly against the walls on either side. I used a thick piece of wood moulding as a base. A hearth which extends further forward would, again, take up too much space.

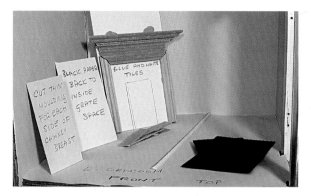

This striking, Dutch-style fireplace has a surround fitted with replica Delft tiles. The plaster roundel above the fireplace and an elaborate tulip vase complete the effect.

## Making a fire

An empty grate can look rather blank and unfriendly. It is easy to make a cheerful-looking fire, by the method given below, to create a homely atmosphere. Alternatively, why not put a miniature dried flower arrangement in the grate for a fresh, summery look?

A glowing fire is simple and quick to make. A purchased grate (or one made from a kit) can be fitted, or a piece of wood will make a perfect base for the fire, which can be placed directly in the hearth.

### Method

- Small piece of wood approximately ⅜in (10mm) thick
- Railway modeller's coal *or* a few small twigs
- Tube of red glitter
- Scraps of red cellophane and gold paper

### Materials

1  Cut the wood to fit at the base of the fireplace, or inside a purchased grate. Paint the wood matt black, or use a black marker pen to colour it.
2  Cover alternately with all-purpose glue and coal, building up a good shape with several layers. Use twigs instead for a log fire.
3  Dab the arrangement with a little more glue and sprinkle generously with red glitter.
4  Add 'flames' at the back by gluing on small twists of the red cellophane and gold paper. One of each will probably be enough.
5  Allow the glue to set firm and then give the fire a tap to dislodge any loose glitter before placing it in the grate or on the hearthstone.

## Staircases

### Balusters

Some houses will be fitted with a staircase complete with balusters and handrail but if yours is a basic flight of steps, you can add these extras yourself without too much trouble. Lengths of handrail, newel posts and packets of balusters are inexpensive and can be purchased from dolls' house suppliers. The handrail will have a groove cut on the underside to take the balusters. The balusters are often turned, but if you want a simpler and plainer look, perhaps for an early-Georgian house, you could use ⅛in (3mm) square dowelling as 'stick' balusters.

### Materials

- 1/12-scale handrails, newel posts and balusters, in the style and quantity required (allow 1 baluster for each step)
- Paint or varnish (white-painted balusters with mahogany or pine-stained posts and handrail look stylish)

The newel posts, balusters and handrail for this staircase are generally available in dolls' house shops. The effect was enhanced by a dado rail with white paint below and a cool green above. A wallpaper border accentuates the scheme.

1 Before fitting, paint or varnish the balusters, newel posts and handrail in your desired style. Make sure everything has dried properly before moving on to the next stage.

2 Fit the top and bottom newel posts first, using all-purpose adhesive. Check with a set square that they are vertical and leave overnight for the glue to set.

3 Cut the handrail to size, cutting the ends at an angle to fit between the newel posts, and glue in place.

4 To fit the balusters, cut the top of each at an angle to slot into the groove in the handrail. You may need to whittle away a little at the top for a neat fit. Glue in place.

This may all sound complicated, but once you start you will find that it is straightforward, if a little fiddly.

## Side panel

For a modern house, or one which has been updated and is not strictly in period, you may wish to put in a side panel instead of balusters for the stairs.

- ¼in (6mm) square dowelling
- Firm card
- Thin wood (jelutong is suitable, or you could use rigid cardboard)
- Paint or varnish
- Wooden beading (optional)

1 Cut newel posts from the square dowelling and glue in as in the previous method. An average post would be 3–4in (76–102mm) high, but this will depend on the ceiling heights in your house.

2 Cut a card pattern for the side panel and try for size before cutting the thin wood to the correct measurements. The panel should be about 2½in (64mm) tall and long enough to fit neatly between the

newel posts. The ends will need to be cut at an angle to enable the panel to fit properly up the slope of the stairs (*see* diagram 1). The average dolls' house staircase is steeper than a real one, so the angle is likely to be 45°.

3 Check that the wooden panel will fit correctly and paint or varnish it to match the surrounding decorations. Leave to dry and then glue in place (*see* diagram 2). If the hall and staircase are to be wallpapered, you can paper over the panel too, but this should be done *after* fitting, along with the rest of the decoration.

4 To make a neat edge at the base of the panel, glue a strip of thin wooden beading along the bottom, between the newel posts.

**Fitting a side panel for a staircase.**

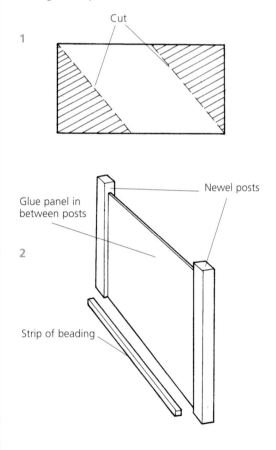

## Boxed-in staircase

Some dolls' house staircases are boxed in between the outer house wall and the adjacent room. In this case you might like to fit a rope handrail.

### Method

1   Fit the picture screws into the outside wall at the top and bottom of the staircase, at a suitable height above the stairs.
2   Thread the silk cord through the eyes of the screws, up the length of the staircase, finishing with a decorative loop at each end.
3   Stitch through the cord to secure firmly in place.

**A non-opening door at the rear of this small dining room gives the impression of a hall beyond. The room has been made a more interesting shape by bringing part of the back wall forward to create a recess for the door (by gluing a piece of MDF or polyboard approximately ¾in [19mm] thick to the back wall).**

## Stairs are not essential

A basic staircase is fitted in most dolls' houses, but in a small two-room house, for example, stairs are sometimes omitted to save space. In this case, you can give the impression that there is a staircase out of sight by fitting a purchased internal door (non-opening) to the back wall. Paint the door before fitting and simply glue it on to the wall, fairly near one corner. It is worth making a proper door surround as well, in order to make this arrangement appear realistic (*see* page 62).

# Flooring

## Carpet

The simplest of all floor coverings for a dolls' house is fitted carpet. Self-adhesive felt with a peel-off backing is available in a limited colour range (from dolls' house stockists and haberdashers), but you will have a wider choice if you use fine woollen, woollen-mixture, or velvet dress fabrics. Colours which are very dark or very bright will tend to swamp the contents of any room: a medium tone or simple pattern will give the best effect. Lay all carpet after the decorating is complete and the skirting boards have been fitted. Double-sided adhesive tape is the best thing to use for fixing the carpet down.

### Fixed hard flooring

As an attractive alternative to carpet, various types of fixed hard flooring could be used in some rooms. A parquet floor for the sitting room, black and white tiles for the hall, and quarry tiles or flagstones for the kitchen, are all possibilities and can be laid in a single piece. Sheets of fibreglass cladding representing these materials can be cut with a craft knife or scissors and glued directly on to the wooden floors of the house with PVA white wood glue. Hard flooring should be fitted before skirting boards are glued in place.

**Easy to apply fibreglass sheets make dealing with flooring a simple matter. Yellow quarry tiles, black-and-white tile effect and parquet flooring would be suitable for kitchen, hall and sitting room.**

## Joins

The join between two different types of flooring in adjacent rooms can look untidy. Copy the method used in full-size houses and cover the join with thin brass strip, available from hobby shops. It can be cut to size easily, using a small saw, and glued in place.

## Cutting patterns for fixed flooring

The most fail-safe way of making sure your hard flooring fits perfectly is to cut a paper pattern first. This avoids unfortunate mistakes when cutting the fibreglass sheets, and, if you keep the paper patterns, they can save some fiddly measuring if you decide to refurbish at a later date. Use fairly stiff paper for the patterns. Uncreased brown paper or salvaged photocopying paper is ideal.

### Method

1. Measure the room size and cut a piece of paper about 1in (25mm) larger all round than the finished size of the flooring.
2. Lay the paper on the floor of the room, with one edge along the front edge of the room. Crease the paper to fit the sides and back of the room before cutting; snip and fold at awkward corners to get a good fit. If there are tricky joins or alcoves, add an extra piece of paper and join with adhesive tape.

3. Trim the pattern carefully. Check that it fits exactly and make any final adjustments. Write 'top' and 'front' clearly on the pattern to avoid mistakes when using it to cut the flooring material itself.

## Realism

Real wooden planking, flagstones or Victorian-style tiles are more expensive than sheet flooring as they are individually made. They also take time to fit, but are worth the effort involved for the effect they give. For details of how to fit these more specialist materials, see Chapter 11.

## Paper floors

Paper printed to simulate a variety of flooring materials is also available from dolls' house stockists, but it is not hard-wearing. A paper floor is nonetheless a good temporary measure while you decide on something more permanent. Paper cut-outs of oriental carpets from magazines, for example, can look surprisingly effective on a dolls' house floor. Even brown paper can represent a wooden floor in a small room – use semi-matt Kraftpaper, the type which has small lines.

**Samples of suitable paper flooring materials.**

# Internal doors

Doors between rooms are not essential in a dolls' house and they are sometimes supplied as optional extras with both finished houses and kits. A simple archway or opening between the rooms has the advantage of making the house seem lighter and more spacious.

If you do want to put in internal doors, you can fit them yourself, but it is not the easiest of tasks unless you have some woodwork experience. Care is needed to make sure the doors are hung perfectly straight. Another potential obstacle is that, if the hinges are to scale, the screws will be so tiny that dealing with them is extremely fiddly (and if dropped, they may never be found). Manufacturers of dolls' house kits sometimes supply oversize hinges and screws, which are much easier for the amateur to manage. The result is inevitably less elegant but more practical.

In general, I am happy to omit internal doors in the interests of light. I also like the way in which, by looking through a doorway, different views of the rooms are opened up. I decided to fit internal doors in my interior design shop, however, as everything is arranged so that the displays look best from the front.

### Method

1 First check that the door is the right way up. On a four-panel door the longer panels go at the top; on a six-panel door the smallest panels go at the top. Plan to fit the door so that it opens into the room and away from the front of the house. This will make it easier to see through into the room on the other side of the door.

2 Make sure that the hinges are the right way round so that the door will open. Drill holes and screw the hinges on to the door first.

3 Holding the door in place, mark the position for the other side of the hinges on the door frame, then drill the holes and screw into place.

4 Paint or varnish the doors before fitting.

### Keeping screws safe

Keep the screws in an eggcup while fitting the hinges, and use tweezers to pick them up. 'Partpicker' tweezers with a magnifier attached may be helpful.

Fit doorknobs before fixing the doors in place, so that it can be done with the door laid flat.

## Fitting doors the easy way

Unless the house is to be played with by young children, it is a good idea to substitute smaller, neater brass hinges for the ones provided, omit screws altogether, and simply glue the hinges in place with superglue. This solution avoids the out-of-scale look of oversize hinges, and the door will not be prevented from closing properly by large screw-heads.

## Cloth hinges

Cloth hinges are a suitable alternative for a child's dolls' house. They will not be invisible, but are reasonably neat and serviceable. Children enjoy being able to open and shut doors in a dolls' house to add realism to their games and cloth hinges can be replaced easily if the door is accidentally pulled off.

### Method

1 Cut a narrow strip of cotton tape or seam binding just shorter than the height of the door.

2 Fold the tape firmly and accurately in half lengthwise, and iron in the crease.

3 Using all-purpose adhesive, glue the folded tape first to the door edge and then to the edge of the door frame on one side of the aperture, just as for normal hinges (*see* diagram overleaf).

**Fitting a cloth hinge to an internal door.**

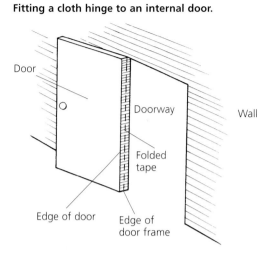

Door

Doorway

Wall

Folded tape

Edge of door

Edge of door frame

# Interior decoration

## Painting

Once the features detailed above have been fitted, it is time to start the main decoration. Painting the interior walls with emulsion paint is the quickest and easiest method. Cover floors before you begin and always apply two coats of paint to the walls to avoid any patchiness showing up later.

Door and window frames should be undercoated and painted *before* fitting if possible (*see* page 62). If they are already fitted, paint them before decorating the walls.

It is always a good rule to start at the back wall of a room and work forwards, to avoid the danger of smudging a newly painted area with the back of your hand.

### Light

It is important to work in a good light so that you can see exactly what you are doing. It is worth using an anglepoise or table lamp to allow you to see properly into the back corners. A torch will make a good temporary spotlight.

## Painting a stairwell

Fixed stairs always make decorating more difficult, especially if they are narrow, steep and enclosed. The easiest way to paint a very narrow upper hall is to do as much as can be reached conveniently with a brush (*see* picture), and then sponge the paint on into the more inaccessible area on the side and back walls, using a small sponge attached to a paint stick with a rubber band. Take care not to oversaturate the sponge with emulsion, and cover the stairs with masking tape to avoid splashes while painting. Balusters and handrail, etc. can be protected with paper or masking tape as well.

**Painting a stairwell is an awkward and fiddly business. Care must be taken to achieve a smooth covering of paint.**

### Paintbrushes

Do not throw away old art paintbrushes. Cut off the brush end and keep the wooden part as a paint stick: it will be useful for stirring paints and as an aid to decorating awkward areas such as stairwells.

Another difficulty with fixed-in stairs is how to deal with the zigzag shape where the edge of the treads meets the wall. Using a ruler, draw a pencil line on the wall down the side of the stairs and finish the emulsion paint above the line (*see* picture below). Paint (or varnish) below the line to match the stair treads and/or skirting boards and then glue on a strip of beading to cover the line itself. This method can also be followed when using wallpaper (*see* page 61).

**A strip of thin beading will be glued on to cover the join between the white paint and the emulsion or wallpaper above the zigzag line.**

**A selection of regular and miniaturized wallpapers. It is difficult to tell by appearance alone which is which. The regular ones are thicker and will not stretch when pasted. Remnants of patterned wallpaper can be useful: use part of the design for the walls and create a complementary border, perhaps from a stripe. Piecing is not difficult on such a small scale.**

# Wallpaper

Dolls' house wallpaper is supplied in separate pieces (rather than on a roll). Allow one piece for each wall. In practice it is wise to buy an extra sheet to allow for pattern repeats or wastage. Measure all the walls before you go shopping, and remember to allow for chimney breasts and doorways, which may involve joins.

Ordinary giftwrap is cheaper than specially made wallpaper and comes in much larger sheets. Occasionally you can find the perfect design for your room at the stationer's, so it is worth keeping an eye open. Here again, I would still buy an extra sheet, just in case of accidents. If it is not needed for the dolls' house, you can always use it later for its intended purpose.

### Applying wallpaper

Some wallpapers which have been specially designed in 1/12 scale are very thin, and will stretch alarmingly if overwetted. The thicker the paper, the easier it is to paste up. It is worth looking also at regular wallpapers with small patterns, as these are often suitable.

## Using a paper pattern

As with fixed hard flooring (*see* page 78), you will find it easier to cut a paper pattern first before cutting the wallpaper itself. Again use fairly stiff paper, and cut a separate pattern for each wall. The pattern for each side wall should extend by about ⅛in (3mm) to fit round the corner and on to the back wall. The side walls should be papered first and the back, cut exactly to size, can then be fitted over neatly to make an almost invisible join and avoid any possibility of a gap. If the edges are to be concealed behind skirtings, cornices or borders, the paper need not fit exactly to the top and bottom of the walls.

If you need to fit paper round a door which is situated near a corner, it is best to make a join at the top of the door. A separate piece can then be used for the small area above and to the side of the door (*see* diagram overleaf).

This will avoid the danger of tearing the fragile strip of paper while trying to hang a piece for the whole wall. If you have fitted a chimney breast, you will need to plan a join either side of it.

**The best way to paper between a door and the wall.**

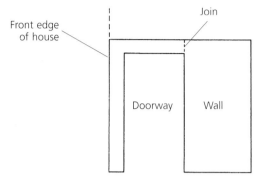

When you cut out the wallpaper pieces from your patterns, make sure that the design is the right way up and that any repeat pattern will match at the joins, allowing for the ⅛in (3mm) overlap at the back corners. Write 'left', 'right' and 'back' in pencil lightly on the reverse of the appropriate piece, with an arrow pointing to the top, to avoid mistakes when applying.

## Paperhanging

Hanging wallpaper in a dolls' house is much easier than in a full-size house, but care is still needed, particularly if you are using special 1/12-scale paper. The important thing is to take your time: make sure that you are placing the wallpaper accurately, and take care to avoid depositing stray smears of paste.

### Method

1    Mix up some regular wallpaper paste according to the maker's instructions. If you are using 1/12-scale paper, you will need to make the paste slightly thinner.
2    Size (or prepare) the walls first by pasting over them, and leave to dry for about half an hour, or until dry to the touch.
3    Paste each piece of wallpaper thoroughly immediately before hanging, making sure

that the paste reaches right to the edges. You will need to hang the side walls first and the back wall last.

4    For each side wall, line up the front edge first, to avoid the need for fiddly trimming later. Smooth the paper over the whole wall, and press gently all over with a piece of screwed-up soft kitchen or toilet paper. Use a fresh piece to smooth over each wall, to avoid accidental trails of paste.

5    Do not panic if your newly applied wallpaper seems to be full of bubbles and lumps. This is part of the drying out process: just forget it until the next day. Save the left-over paste and, if you find that any corners or front edges have not adhered properly, you can stick them down using a small brush to work the paste under the edge.

## Papering the entire opening front

Covering the inside of the opening front is more tricky than papering a room, as you will need to circumvent a fair number of windows and one or two doorways. The easiest method is to paper straight over the apertures. Leave until the next day, when the paper will be thoroughly dried out, and cut carefully round the edges of the windows and doorways with a craft knife. You will find that this is easy to do neatly.

A wallpaper with a plain border has been fitted instead of curtains or blinds, to emphasize windows and floor divisions on the inside of a three-storey, eighteenth-century house.

For a small house, one piece of paper will be sufficient to cover the entire opening front. You can use a different paper for each floor, but the general effect is likely to be more attractive if you choose a single design which will complement all the interior decorations.

If you need to join sheets of paper at any point, try to place the join at the edge of a window, where it will be less noticeable.

**The opening front of my interior design shop was almost double-depth for the wallpaper I had chosen. I used wallpaper border, strategically placed to attract attention to the window display and to disguise the join across.**

## Papering the staircase and hall

It is not at all easy to wallpaper around a fixed-in staircase, especially if it has a half-landing and second flight of stairs leading up from the back. If you are sure you want to use wallpaper rather than emulsion paint for this area, choose a paper where there is no need to match the pattern. A marbled or mottled effect will be easier to fit. I used a large sheet of hand-marbled paper bought at a craft fair for the staircase in my eighteenth-century shop (*see* the picture above right). It was even thicker than regular wallpaper, so I could slide it around the awkward angles of the staircase without any risk of tearing.

Using a marble-effect paper solves another potential difficulty. The base of the wall at the back of a half-landing will be almost inaccessible, and fitting skirtings to such an area is virtually impossible. Skirting boards are not strictly necessary with a marble wall, and I

**In the eighteenth century, the use of marbled wallpaper became popular, to simulate expensive real marble. If the paper is chosen carefully, it can look impressive, but is perhaps rather ostentatious for the smaller home. A large house or a shop is the ideal situation.**

prefer the simpler effect when the 'marble' joins the floor with no adornment.

Fit the wallpaper against the staircase edge on the side wall using the method described on page 59 for painting the same area: the wallpaper should finish above the pencil line as the emulsion paint would. You can then paint or varnish below the line as appropriate, and add a strip of beading along the join.

## Wallpaper borders

A pretty border along the top of a plain wall will make a neat finish and is equally effective whether used with a plain wallpaper or over emulsion paint. Scaled-down designs are available to complement 1/12-scale wallpapers. It is worth checking out other sources for suitable borders, from advertising leaflets to full-size wallpaper borders, where part of the pattern can be selected for miniature use by judicious cutting.

Borders can be used with or instead of

cornices. They can also be used to provide an attractive frame for a door or window instead of wood, or in place of a wooden dado or picture rail.

A selection of borders to enhance plain walls: one is cut out from a supermarket leaflet, while the others include a 1/12-scale border and two trimmed from regular wallpaper borders. They can also be used to surround doors or windows, or in place of a dado rail.

### Method

1 Cut a separate length of border for each wall, making sure that the pattern will match where it is to be joined at or near the corners. It is best to butt the pieces together with no overlap.

2 Paste one length at a time, wait for a minute and then apply. Do the side walls first, lining up the front edge carefully to avoid the need for trimming later.

3 Be careful when applying the pasted length of border to the already decorated wall: do not allow one end to trail, but use one hand to press gently along the length while the other hand keeps the rest of the paper under control.

4 Smooth over carefully with screwed-up kitchen or toilet paper as in the method for papering walls (*see* page 60).

# Fittings

To add the finishing touches to your interior decoration, skirtings, cornices, door and window frames need to be fitted.

# Door frames

Whether or not you have chosen to fit internal doors, a door frame can give a finished appearance to an opening between rooms. It will also cover the wallpaper edges or make a neat finish to emulsion paint round the doorway. All you need do is cut three pieces of wood moulding, using the same method as for mitring corners on fireplace mouldings (*see* page 49). Paint the wood as required and glue in place around the door or opening. As an alternative to wood moulding, use braid trim to make a surround.

## Skirtings, cornices, dado and picture rails

All these fittings are optional, but as well as being historically correct for some period houses, they have the advantage of concealing edges where, in the miniature scale, it is difficult to make a perfect join.

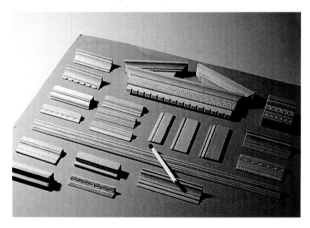

Replica wooden mouldings provide accurate period detail in a Georgian, Victorian or modern room. The broken pediment can be used over a doorway or to top a bookcase (*see* page 85).

Scaled down wooden mouldings suitable for these fittings are supplied in 18in (45.7cm) lengths, or occasionally 12in (30.5cm) only. When you measure up, remember to allow extra so that the ends of each piece can be mitred to join at the corners of the rooms, and also at the edges of any chimney breasts. It is worth buying an extra length in any case, to allow for mitres, mistakes and any change of arrangement during fitting. You might also want to practise cutting mitres on a spare piece. Left-over short lengths are always useful for making up fireplaces (*see* page 50).

All these fittings are best lightly glued in with all-purpose adhesive, not PVA wood glue, as they do not need to be fixed permanently in place. You may wish to remove the fittings for redecoration at a later date.

### Avoiding joins

Always use one complete piece of moulding along each wall. A join is never satisfactory as it always shows when painted, however carefully it is fitted and sanded.

## Skirtings

Thin stripwood is economical for skirtings and can simply be butted together at the corners of the room. This method is also very suitable for children's dolls' houses (*see* page 35).

To fit scaled down replicas of period-style skirtings, it is worth taking the trouble to learn how to cut a mitre for the joins. Most modern homes have skirting boards, so that you can check on the real thing to see how the pieces fit together.

Many dolls' houses have internal doorways sited very close to the front of the house, so there will be a wall space of only about ½in (13mm) long between the front opening edge of the house and the side of the door frame. In theory this gap should also have skirting fitted, but in practice such a small piece will look messy and it is better to omit it.

### Method

1   To cut a mitred join in replica wooden moulding, place the plain back of the moulding upright against the back of the mitre box (*see* diagram), in the same position as it will be fitted against the wall in the house. (Note that this position differs from that used when cutting moulding for

fireplaces, door and window frames.)

2   Cut the mouldings for the rear wall first and check the fit.

3   Next cut the pieces for each side wall. Cut the mitre first and, when you are sure that this fits neatly, cut off the excess length at the front. Identify each piece in pencil on the reverse.

4   Paint or varnish as required and leave to dry thoroughly.

5   Glue in place.

**The correct angle for cutting mitred corners in wood moulding for skirting boards.**

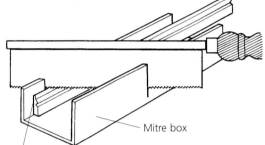

Plain back of moulding upright — Mitre box

### Mitred joins

The angle for cutting mitred joins is the same for skirtings, cornices, dado and picture rails (*see* Method above), but different for fireplaces, door, window and picture frames (*see* pages 49, 62, 65 and 96). You will soon have this clear in your mind if you try comparing the relative positions of the moulding on a skirting board and a fireplace.

## Cornices

Cornices were a standard fitting in rooms during the eighteenth and nineteenth centuries. A large, impressive cornice might have been used in the main rooms, with more modest ones in the bedrooms and service rooms. Prepare and fit as for skirtings. A wallpaper border can be used to define the top edge of the wall instead or in addition (*see* page 64). Lace trimming is a pretty and simple alternative: all you need to do is glue it in place.

**A wallpaper border and dado rail add emphasis to this large room. The angle of the cut for dado and cornice to fit the corners of a chimney breast is exactly the opposite to that used in the corner of a room on these fittings. On the chimney breast the joins project outwards into the room instead of fitting together in a corner.**

## Dado rails

A dado rail will help to give the correct appearance to a Georgian room, but is best omitted from a very small house where it will create too many divisions. If present, it should be placed at about one-third of the height of the room (it was originally intended to be level with the back of an upright chair, to prevent it marking the wall). It can also mark a change in pattern or wall colour, with a plain surface below the rail and wallpaper above, or a darker colour below and a paler one above.

## Picture rails

You might want to fit picture rails in a 1930s or '40s house. In a dolls' house room with a wall height of 10 or 11in (25.4 or 27.9cm), for example, the picture rail should be placed

### Keeping rails level

In practice, not all dolls' house walls are exactly straight. The simplest way to fit a dado rail accurately is to decide how high above the floor it is to be placed and cut a piece of card about 2in (5cm) wide to match this height. Keeping the lower end of the card against the floor, move it along the wall and draw a fine pencil line along the top as you continue round the room. Check that the lines meet at the corners and double-check that the height matches at the front edges. For a picture rail, use the same method but measure down from the ceiling. The pencil line will indicate where to end wallpaper and begin emulsion paint, if the style of decoration is to be different above and below, and the dado or picture rail can then be glued on to conceal the join.

about 1½in (38mm) from the ceiling. Whatever the style of decoration on the walls, the area of wall above the picture rail should be coloured to match the ceiling.

# Windows

## Window glazing

Windows are often supplied with the dolls' house – already screen-printed with white glazing bars or black, diamond-shaped panes to suit the style of the house – and instructions for fitting them will be provided.

If you have to make your own windows, use plain acetate (available from hobby shops). The sheets are about 8 x 10in (20.3 x 25.4cm) and are protected on both sides by a peel-off film to prevent them being scratched before use.

### Cutting acetate

Take extra care when cutting with a craft knife and metal raised-edge ruler, as acetate is very slippery. The knife blade can easily skate over the surface if not held firmly. Acetate of the correct weight is a little too thick to cut comfortably and neatly using scissors.

### Method

1    Remove the protective film from the acetate sheet. Cut the acetate ¼in (6mm) larger all round than the window space so that it will overlap on each edge.
2    Apply a tiny amount of all-purpose glue to the wall around the window aperture. Leave for a few seconds to become tacky.
3    Press the glazing gently into place. *Do not* slide it about, or the glue will leave a trail on the clean surface.

### Removing glue

Keep an orange stick and some white spirit handy while fitting glazing. If you smear some glue on the acetate by accident you can wipe it off if you act immediately. This should not occur if you are economical with the glue and wait until it is tacky before fixing the acetate in place.

## Window frames

Complete internal window frames are not necessary if you plan to add curtains and pelmets (*see* page 80), but to make the window look finished it is usually best to glue on a thin strip of wood below it to form a windowsill. If you plan to fit blinds (*see* page 81), add thin stripwood or moulding at the sides and a sill at the bottom. There is no need to mitre any corners: it is simplest to make the sill extend slightly beyond the side frames.

## Shop windows

A shop window needs a complete frame inside as there will be no curtains. Mitre the corners of the wooden mouldings as described for fireplace mouldings (*see* page 49). Surround with a wallpaper border for an extra decorative feature and to finish everything off with a flourish.

### Clearance

Before adding window frames, check that there is sufficient clearance for them when the house is closed up. If windows are sited near the front edge of one of the room walls, the addition of a frame, or even a curtain, might prevent the house from closing properly. In this case, edge the window with a wallpaper border instead (*see* page 61).

# 9 *Special paint finishes*

If you enjoy playing with colour, it is possible to create some stunning effects with a bit of imagination. You need not stick with the paint colours specified on shade cards, but can mix and match until you have just the result you want. Be adventurous in mixing different kinds of paint: some of the most interesting tones and finishes can be achieved by mixing emulsion with gouache or model paint.

**Black-and-white half-timbered houses look spectacular. Nonetheless, a more subtle effect will be achieved with pink or ochre walls and natural oak beams, in line with modern thoughts on conservation. I used chestnut stain for the beams on this house, which show up well without being too dark.**

Professional interior decorators are often fond of rag-rolling, stencilling and sponging, and these techniques are equally effective in 1/12 scale, both for interior and exterior use. The techniques mentioned below are simply examples of what can be done. They may well spark off other ideas for you.

## Exterior paint effects

### Walls

Houses in cob or plaster are often colour-washed, and such effects are not difficult to reproduce in 1/12 scale. The best way to achieve a suitably warm, intense colour is to mix normal emulsion paint with gouache. The example given below creates the colour I used for my Kentish Wealden house *(see* picture). The warm ochre colour used for this would be suitable for a cottage or farmhouse too, or you can use the same technique with different colours to suit your particular dolls' house.

### Adjacent surfaces

If you need to paint and varnish on adjacent surfaces, for example on a half-timbered house, apply the varnish first. You can paint over varnish if there is a smudge in the wrong place, but you cannot varnish over a spot of paint.

- 1 tube of yellow ochre gouache
- 1 tube sandstone gouache
- Magnolia emulsion (enough for undercoat and top coat)
- 1in (25mm) paintbrush (preferably already used, as it needs to be stiff – a square-ended stencil brush is equally suitable)
- Small piece of cotton rag
- Matt varnish

**Method**

1   Apply a base coat of emulsion to the exterior walls. Also paint a small piece of wood or firm card as a test.
2   Mix a very small amount of both the yellow ochre and the sandstone gouache into half a pint (0.25l) of the magnolia emulsion. Test the colour on the base-coated card. If necessary, adjust the colour to your liking and then thin the mixture with a very small amount of water.
3   Begin painting on the back of the house to judge the effect. The emulsion/gouache mixture is water soluble so that, if you are not satisfied with the colour after all, you can wipe it off with a damp rag and adjust the mix before starting again.
4   Once you are entirely happy with the colour, paint one wall at a time and immediately rub some of the fresh paint off with a dry rag. A slightly patchy effect is what you want to achieve for a natural-looking finish, with some of the base coat showing through. It is important to work quickly, painting and rubbing each wall in turn, as the mix dries rapidly.
5   Finish with a coat of matt varnish to seal the colour and make it waterproof. This will darken the shade slightly: if you want to check the finished colour first, you will need to varnish the test card too, before painting the walls of the house. You will almost certainly find, however, that the slight darkening is not enough to worry about.

# Roofs

A strong colour can be a good choice for a roof. The one on my Wealden house was copied from a painting of a Kentish house in sunlight, which made the reddish-brown tiles glow a bright orange. This colour was also made up using gouache, this time with a bright orange and a little yellow ochre mixed with

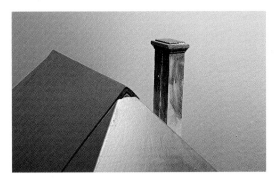

Above **The vibrant colour of the roof of the Wealden house was achieved by using a gouache mix.**

Below **This Cotswold house roof was painted using the same method as for the Wealden house. A mix of buff emulsion, olive-green and mid-grey gouache was used over a buff emulsion basecoat, to complement the warm yellow 'stone' walls.**

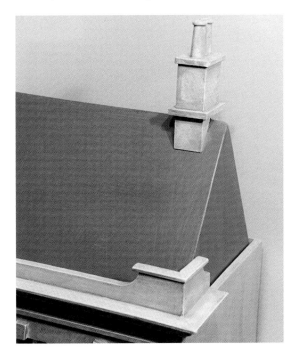

magnolia emulsion. The chimney was painted with the same basic mix as the walls but with some brown added to give a smoke-darkened effect. Use the technique described on page 67 to mix whatever colour you wish for the roof.

## Textured finishes

If you want to create an effect on the exterior walls of your house which goes beyond mere colour, there are a number of ways to add texture. Two are described below.

### Pebble dash

Pebble dash was a highly popular finish for suburban houses built in England, especially during the 1930s and '40s. To reproduce the effect, glue sheets of coarse sandpaper (grade 2½) to the walls, rough side outwards, and paint over them with white or pale grey emulsion. Before painting, conceal joins using interior filler applied with an orange stick.

### Cob or plaster

Originally a building material made of clay and chopped straw, cob can be replicated as an effect on a 1/12-scale cottage.

Textured masonry paint, used to paint and weatherproof real house walls, is ideal for use on small-scale properties, but unless you already have some (perhaps left over from full-scale decorations) a large can will be unnecessarily expensive. It is possible to make up your own textured paint by mixing interior plaster filler with white emulsion paint, diluted with a very small amount of water. The magic extra ingredient is PVA white wood glue. Stir in a small amount to make your mixture bond with the house wall and never flake off. This finish is *permanent* and cannot be removed. Try a test piece on spare wood first.

## Interior paint effects

Emulsion paint in well chosen colours is the quickest method of decorating internal walls. In the house pictured on page 1, I used subtle shades, selected as suitable backgrounds against which furniture and ornaments could be displayed. You need not stick to plain emulsion throughout the house, however, and you might like to try out one or more of the special effects detailed below, to liven up the interior.

## Stencilling

Stencilling has been popular in real-life houses for some years, and a plain wall can be brightened up enormously by the judicious use of stencilled designs. In the miniature scale, it is best to keep such applied decoration to a minimum, because too much stencilling will look far too busy in such a small space. A border round the room, or a simple design on just one wall will give the best effect.

**Whether the stencilling is real or, as in this case, fake – where part of a wallpaper design has been used – emphasize the design by placing the decorative border above a picture rail.**

Cutting out your own stencils in 1/12 scale is tricky. Unless you are unusually dextrous with small tools and have unlimited patience, I recommend buying a miniature stencil, ready-made in brass. Fix the stencil with removable tape while colouring in, using a small paintbrush and stencil paints (also available in tiny sizes for miniaturists).

## Crayons

Waterproof pencil crayons (available from art shops) can be used for stencilling as an easy and less messy alternative to paint. There is a wide range of soft, pastel colours and the appearance of the finished design will look just as good. Sharpen the crayons frequently as a blunt tip will not reach into the corners of a tiny stencil design.

Marbling and other paint effects transform the plaster fireplace, pillars and architrave in this exotic Chinese room.

### Cheat a little

You can achieve an effect that is similar to stencilling by using sections of wallpaper border. The running design used in the room pictured on page 68 makes a good border.

# Marbling

A painted marble effect is a more interesting alternative to using marbled paper for small decorative items, a table top, or fireplace inset. If your house is grand enough to have pillars in the entrance hall, they can also be marbled using this method.

It is best to work with a picture of real marble in front of you as an example. You will

probably want to try a few practice pieces first to get the hang of the technique. A delicately veined marble will look most realistic, so take care not to be too heavy-handed with the paintbrush. You will need model paint in your chosen colours, and a very fine brush.

For the urn pictured on the left I used a base coat of cream model paint. The veining is lightly painted in (feathered) using mid-green and yellow model paint. For the lighter patches, the green is mixed with cream.

# Verdigris

A verdigris finish, to resemble the patina on old copper, brass or bronze, adds an antique character to miniature urns, tubs and garden statues. Miniature terracotta pots make a good base as the paint dries in a matter of minutes on this material and you need not wait between stages. The same paint mix can also be used on the roof of a garden building or the canopy over the balcony of a Regency house.

It took only a few minutes to transform a plain, turned wooden urn by painting it to resemble marble.

### Materials

- 1 sample pot of pale blue emulsion
- 1 small can of model paint in each of the following colours: deep blue, lime green, mid-blue and metallic bronze

Above **Work in progress: three stages in achieving a verdigris finish on metal and terracotta.**

Left **The finished urn looks very different from the original terracotta, with a patina resembling weathered bronze.**

## Method

1   Apply a base coat of the pale blue emulsion to your chosen miniature pot.
2   Once the base coat is dry, apply a coat of bronze model paint, making sure that it covers any ornamentation thoroughly.
3   Mix two different blue-green shades as follows:
    **Mix A (dark)**
    1 dessertspoon of pale blue emulsion
    A few drops each of lime green, deep blue, and mid-blue model paint
    Stir thoroughly, try on paper and adjust the proportions if necessary until you have a bright, greeny-turquoise.
    **Mix B (light)**
    1 dessertspoon of pale blue emulsion
    A few drops each of mid-blue and lime green model paint
    Again stir thoroughly and test. Adjust as necessary to make a paler shade than Mix A.
4   Paint Mix A over the bronze, rubbing off with a paper kitchen towel so that the bronze shows through patchily.
5   Check that the paint is dry, then paint over some parts of the piece with Mix B, again partly rubbing off so that varying degrees of bronze and Mix A show through.

# Silver-blue effect

'Gustavian-style' furniture, which first became popular in eighteenth-century Sweden, seems to be enjoying something of a revival at present. It will add a touch of glamour to a 1/12-scale period room just as it will to an ultra-modern interior.

Paint simple, plain furniture by the same method as for verdigris given above, using silver (metallic) model paint instead of bronze. To alter the appearance of the plain X-frame stool below, I mixed pale blue emulsion first with dark blue model paint for Mix A, and then with pale blue model paint for Mix B.

The top of the repainted X-frame stool is covered with blue-and-white striped cotton and trimmed with narrow braid in a complementary colour, in the approved Swedish fashion.

# 10 *Exterior features*

Chapter 9 set out some options for special paint finishes for house exteriors, both in terms of colour and texture. As an alternative to painting, there are other ways of adding interest to the exterior.

Walls can be finished with sheets of cladding, providing instant wall-hung tiles, weatherboarding (siding) or brick, all realistically coloured and textured. Such sheets are readily available from dolls' house stockists and are simple to apply. If you decide to stick to a plainer paint finish for the walls, you could still add a special finish to the roof.

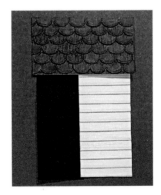

**Shingles, weatherboard (siding) and wall tiles can be fixed quickly and all in one piece.**

## Roofs

A variety of roofing materials are available in sheets similar to the wall claddings. Another option is to use miniature, individual slates and tiles simulated in wood, fibre material or ceramic. These do take time to apply, but are very realistic. The idea of gluing on several hundred miniscule tiles may seem daunting, but

**This handsome, colonial-style American house can be built from a kit which includes rectangular shingles and clapboard siding. The roof space conceals two additional attic rooms.**

once started it does not seem to take long and the end result is highly satisfactory.

## Shingles, slates and tiles

### Shingles

Wooden shingles come in a variety of shapes, so you can choose whichever style suits your dolls' house best. Apply stain before you glue the shingles on. They look best if the depth of colour is varied. Start with the bottom row: each row should overlap the one below by about ¼in (6mm). Stagger the shingles by starting each alternate row with a half-shingle.

If necessary, the shingles can be cut with scissors to fit the rows exactly. Fix on with wood glue.

## Slates

Individual miniature slates are usually made of fibre material in a suitable colour. They are lightweight and easy to fix in the same way as shingles, again using wood glue.

**A selection of slates, tiles and other roof ornaments.**

## Ceramic tiles

Ceramic roof tiles are a more expensive option, but are well worth it to finish off a special dolls' house. I decided to use ceramic Roman roof tiles on my eighteenth-century shop, as I wanted it to match similar shops in Bath, where such tiles are still commonly used. This small roof needed approximately

**These realistic Roman tiles make me think of sunny Italy. They are still one of the standard roofing materials in Bath, which first developed under Roman occupation.**

350 tiles (so beware if you have a large house and limited time). I found them simple to fix, as they have shaped corners so that the overlap slots cleanly into place. Ceramic tiles should be fixed with a rubber-based adhesive.

# Economy option

To achieve the effect of individual plain tiles or slates without any expense, it is possible to make your own, using a railway modeller's method which works just as well on dolls' houses. Slates made of thin card are prepared in strips, rather than individually, and fixed with all-purpose glue. When in place the slates can be painted with acrylic paint and varnished. After painting, you will be delighted with the transformation from humble card to realistic looking slate.

### Method

1  Cut strips of thin card about ½ to ¾in (13 to 19mm) deep, which can be joined to fit the length of the roof. An average strip length might be 8in (20.3cm) but the proportions will depend on the size of your roof.
2  Rule vertical pencil lines on the card strips at ½in (13mm) intervals (*see* diagram 1).

**Cutting the card for inexpensive roof slates.**

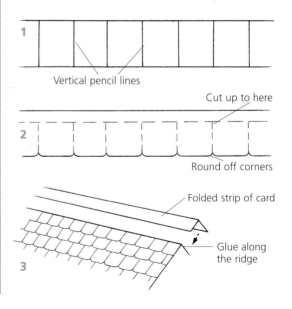

Vertical pencil lines

Cut up to here

Round off corners

Folded strip of card

Glue along the ridge

3  Cut along each pencil line to within about ¼in (6mm) of the top of the strip. (Once the strips are overlapped on the roof, the visible part will resemble a row of slates.) Cut small curves on the lower corners (*see* diagram 2).

4  Glue the strips on to the roof (all-purpose adhesive is best), starting at the bottom and overlapping each row about ¼in (6mm) (as for shingles). Stagger any joins between strips.

5  Finish the top of the roof with a plain strip of card approximately 1½in (38mm) deep, folded in half lengthwise and glued along the ridge to cover the top row of slates (*see* diagram 3).

6  Use acrylic paint to transform the card into realistic-looking slates. A mixture of red, brown and yellow will produce a warm russet colour. Green, grey and yellow will make a pleasing slate grey.

Before you begin painting the roof, make a shade card to keep handy, so that if you have not mixed enough paint it will be easy to match the colour of the next batch correctly. Some slates here and there can be overpainted in a slightly darker shade to give some variation.

7  When the paint is dry, finish with a coat of matt varnish.

| Card |
| --- |
| Save the card stiffeners from shirt or hosiery packaging to make slates. The card is just the right thickness. |

## Thatch

I am often asked how to imitate thatch on a dolls' house, but there is no single solution. There are as many ways of reproducing thatch as there are dolls' house makers and hobbyists who want to try it.

If you are determined to construct a thatch for your dolls' house, the answer is to experiment. Raffia or broom bristles can make a credible thatch: tie the material in bundles and glue these to the roof. If you own a staple gun,

the bundles can be fixed with that. This is a time-consuming process and hard on the hands, although the finished result can be stunning. It helps to work with a picture of a real thatch in front of you as an example.

**This beguiling little cottage is based on one in Sussex: the back extension is weatherboarded and topped by a thatched catslide roof.**

As with slates, start with the bottom row and work upwards, so that each row overlaps the row below. Dormer windows are tricky to work round: cover the section over each dormer separately, before tackling the main roof so that you can make an overlap at the top. Trim the edges neatly to shape with a pair of strong scissors, remembering that thatch always has rounded corners and should overhang the edge of the roof.

## Architectural features

If the outside of your house is too plain for your liking, it can be transformed by the addition of some accurate architectural details in addition to basic wall and roof decoration. It is best to avoid anachronisms by checking up on suitable embellishments for period houses before laying your plans.

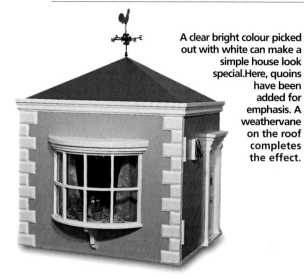

A clear bright colour picked out with white can make a simple house look special. Here, quoins have been added for emphasis. A weathervane on the roof completes the effect.

# Quoins

Quoins are corner bricks used to emphasize the angles at the corners of a square house. They make a smart contrast with brick walls or a plain, painted finish. Ready-cut packs of 'quoining bricks' made from wood are available from dolls' house suppliers, but the quoins on the little house in the picture are of card. They are easily made using the following guidelines.

## Method

1 Measure the height of the house wall and divide the measurement into equal parts to decide on the height of each brick. The exact size will depend on the height of the house, but an average would be 1in (25mm) square for the larger brick and 1 x ½in (25 x 13mm) for the smaller, alternating brick (*see* diagram).

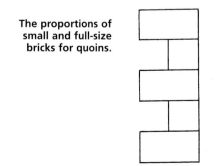

The proportions of small and full-size bricks for quoins.

2 Cut the quoins individually from sturdy card and paint (white, off-white or stone colour) before gluing in place.

# Keystones

Shaped bricks can make an elegant, decorative flourish above the windows of a Georgian, Victorian or Edwardian house (*see* picture, page 75). As with quoins, these, too, can be made very simply in card.

## Method

1 Exact measurements depend on the size of the house. Cut card shapes for each brick similar to those in the diagrams – three keystones for a small house, five for a grander effect.
2 Paint the cards before fixing. Keystones can be white as a contrast on a coloured wall, or brick colour on a brick house. Model paint gives the best finish.

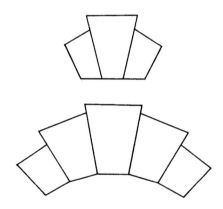

Keystones can be made up either of three or five shaped bricks.

# Chimneys

A good chimney makes all the difference to the appearance of a dolls' house roof. Chimneys can be tall and rectangular (*see* picture, page 75), short and square, with or without pots. If the chimney on your house seems too plain, the easiest thing to do is to add some pots. Contrary to received opinion, chimneypots were installed on many Georgian

**Before and after: it is easy to see the improvement over the original very basic chimney on this roof. The wooden, Tudor-style chimney was made to commission to complete the restoration of an old and dilapidated house.**

houses, although it was during the Victorian period that whole rows of chimneypots became commonplace.

# The entrance door and porch

The front door, with or without a porch, is such an important feature of any house that it is worth taking trouble to make sure that it is of a suitable style and properly decorated.

The pictures below show some fine examples of front doors from houses of different periods. If your house came supplied with a plain front door, it can be improved with the addition of attractive door furniture.

**The texture and colour of ancient stone is mimicked brilliantly in paint. This porch to a gatehouse is based on one at sixteenth-century Montacute House, Somerset.**

**A Georgian doorcase with fanlight and arched pediment, faithfully copied from a seventeenth-century house in Bristol, England. The maker has included the lead flashing over the porch and keystones above the window.**

**A planked oak door nestling under the overhanging, jettied storey of a timber-framed house is meticulously copied from an original building.**

# 11 *Interior features*

Details of individual furnishing items and how to make them, plus ideas for decorative accessories, are given in Chapters 12, 13 and 14. Before getting down to the smaller details, however, you may like to consider building in a larger special feature, beyond the basic fixtures and fittings described in previous chapters. Depending on the style of your house, one or more of the following suggestions may be suitable for you to use.

## Kitchen range recess

A range is the focal point of any Victorian kitchen. It will look even more impressive if it is fitted into a recess, with a chimney breast above and a wide mantelshelf for displaying ornaments. A chimney breast the full width of the kitchen will provide useful storage space either side of the range for a coal scuttle and a kettle on a stand. The following method and pictures should make the construction process clear. (The same method could be used to create a recess for an Aga cooker.)

### Materials

- ½in (13mm) square wooden dowelling
- Thick cardboard
- Wooden moulding (for mantelshelf and side trim)
- Paint, wallpaper and/or tiles as required

### Method

1 Cut three lengths of the square dowelling, one to fit against each side wall, and one to go above them at the top of the wall to make a frame for the recess.
2 Measure the depth of the range and glue dowelling to walls and ceiling ½in (13mm) further forward than this measurement.

**Siting the kitchen range: work in progress.**

3    Cut a piece of thick cardboard the width of the back wall and approximately 3½in (89mm) high. Glue to the top of the wooden surround so that it forms the chimney breast above the range.

4    Paint or wallpaper the card to match the intended decor of the rest of the room.

5    Glue a piece of mantelshelf moulding to the front of the chimney breast at the base of the card, and one piece down each side over the dowelling. The moulding can be stained or painted before gluing in place.

6    Paper the inside of the recess with fake tile paper, or use real tiles for a more realistic effect.

7    The range and any ornaments or cooking utensils can then be placed in the recess.

**The finished kitchen with its built-in range.**

## Inglenook fireplace

The typical wide chimney breast over an open hearth in an old cottage or Tudor house is known as an inglenook, as there was sufficient space on each side of the fire to sit in the 'nook'. Such fireplaces were constructed by incorporating a solid oak beam instead of a mantelshelf over the fireplace.

An inglenook fireplace can be made in the same way as the kitchen range recess. Instead of mantelshelf moulding, glue a piece of oak veneer about 1in (25mm) high to the front of the chimney breast. Before gluing in place, distress the wood slightly by denting it with a small hammer, and stain to resemble darkened oak. Line the fireplace with brick paper or brick cladding.

This brick-lined inglenook fireplace boasts a traditional cast-iron fireback and a rotating spit as well as a pot crane and a hanging griddle tray. Horse brasses, a corn dolly and a bread dough harvest twist all add to the atmosphere of a well-used kitchen.

## Realistic flooring

The guide to basic decoration in Chapter 8 gives simple, economical ideas for a variety of flooring materials (*see* pages 55–6). Here are two more elaborate floor treatments if you want something more realistic. The time and trouble you take will be amply rewarded by the look of the finished room.

These materials will be more expensive than the simpler options, but will last as long as the house and should never need replacing. In terms of colour and texture, using miniature versions of the real thing simply cannot be beaten.

# Flagstones

Ceramic or resin flagstones are ideal for the Tudor or Georgian home, especially for the kitchen (*see* picture, page 77). They are thicker than sheet flooring (*see* page 55) and will need to be cut to fit awkward corners. Ceramic flagstones can be cut with a standard, tungsten-carbide-tipped tile cutter, which will have instructions on the pack. Follow these carefully. Resin flagstones can be cut with a junior hacksaw.

Glue the flagstones on to a card base (cut to the exact shape of the room) or, if you are confident, directly on to the wooden floor of the dolls' house. Use a rubber-based adhesive for ceramic flagstones. Wood glue works best with resin ones and they will also be improved by a coat of satin-finish varnish in a light shade such as pine or light oak (*see* picture page 24).

# Planked flooring

Ready-cut strips of iron-on veneer in oak, pine or mahogany will make realistic planked floors (*see* picture of the Wealden house interior, page 79), although this is a more time-consuming option than sheet flooring. Packs of planking are supplied by dolls' house stockists with instruc-

tions for fitting, but the following hints on fitting and varnishing should help you avoid any pitfalls and produce a satisfactory result.

## Hints for a perfect floor

1   Cut a card pattern for the floor (following the method on page 56) and use this as a base on to which the planks will be fixed (*see* picture below). It is worth painting the surface of the card with watercolour paint of a similar shade to the intended colour of the finished planking so that any minute gaps between planks will not be obvious. The front edge of the card should also be coloured to avoid a white streak showing up when the floor is fixed in place.

Cutting a card pattern for a planked floor.

**To fit an external doorstep, measure, cut and paint a strip of wood and glue to the front of the house or between the edges of the door surround. Make sure that the base is level with the base of the rest of the front, so that it does not catch when the house is opened. It should be thick enough to conceal any small gap which would otherwise show below the door.**

---

### Opening doors

Before you make a final decision on flooring material, check whether any opening doors will allow for the extra thickness on the floor. This can be a problem with the more realistic flooring options such as flagstones.

If the door is likely to scrape along the flooring, or not open at all, unscrew the hinges and cut a thin strip off the base of the door before refitting.

For a front door, this may involve making an extra exterior doorstep (*see* picture opposite) to fill the resulting gap outside. Measure carefully and cut stripwood of a suitable thickness to make a step, or two if necessary. Those in the picture are ⅜in (10mm) high. Paint the step an appropriate colour before gluing in place at the base of the doorway.

2  Miniature planking is supplied in 18in (45.7cm) lengths and will need to be cut to size with scissors or a craft knife. On average, the longest planks should be approximately three-quarters of the length of the room. The planks should be staggered as they would be on a real floor, with short lengths used at the ends or as spacers. Try to keep the pieces in the same order as they were cut, so that when they are laid down and butted together there will be a neat join between each.

3  Floorboards in a real house normally run from front to back because the joists run across, between supporting walls at the sides. In a dolls' house, however, the visual effect is better if the boards run parallel with the front. You can then start with one extra-long plank right across the front to give a clean edge.

4  For a Georgian or Shaker-style house, finish with one or two coats of matt varnish. For other periods, use two, or even three, coats of semi-matt varnish.

## Applying varnish to planking

1  Varnishing requires a slightly different technique from painting. The trick is to imagine that you are floating the varnish over the surface of the wood. I use a ¾in (19mm) brush, or ½in (13mm) for a very small house.

2  Use light, smooth strokes. Never dab at a spot you think you may have missed: wait for the next coat to cover it.

3  Rub down lightly between coats with the finest glasspaper.

4  For a really smooth finish, rub over gently with a soft cloth (not glasspaper) before applying the final coat.

5  Varnish produces strong fumes and it is important to work in a well-ventilated room, with the window open if possible.

6  A dust-free atmosphere is important while the surface is drying, because varnish seems to attract any small particles and these will spoil the finished effect.

**Crooked beams make a surround for an original miniature oil painting. The planked floor in undarkened oak helps to keep the room light.**

# Half-timbering internal walls

Tudor-style dolls' houses are half-timbered on the outside, but the internal walls are usually supplied plain, whether the house is bought ready-made or as a kit. It is rare to find that all the rooms in a genuine Tudor house have been plastered over, so it is a good idea to add some internal timbers to complement those on the outside. You might want to leave one or two rooms without timbering – perhaps the parlour and a bedroom – and decorate these with a stencil design (*see* page 68).

Use thin stripwood (available from hobby shops) and dent this by knocking with a small hammer. Cut the strips slightly crooked: ruler-straight edges will look unnatural. Although in reality such timbers are part of the framework of the house and therefore as thick inside as out, I find it is better to scale the size down a little for the interior if the effect is not to look overdone in such a small space. The main timbers might be ½in (13mm) or ⅝in (15mm) wide and the infill timbers ¼in (6mm) or ⅜in (10mm) wide, but the proportions will vary to suit your particular house: make the timbers whatever width seems to look best. Stain or varnish the timbers to resemble oak before fixing in place with all-purpose glue.

The patterns made by timbering on plain walls are even more effective if you are able to plan in advance where you want to display large pieces of furniture and paintings, because then you can site the timbering to suit your needs perfectly. I always base any internal half-timbering on photographs of real examples. Look at pictures in books or magazines if you cannot go to see the originals.

# 12 *Soft furnishings*

Now that your dolls' house has undergone its basic decoration you can make a start on arranging the interior. Even if you have not yet made or collected very much furniture, the rooms can be softened and made comfortable by the addition of curtains and a few rugs.

## Curtains

Curtains for a dolls' house are easy to make. It is best to choose thin, natural materials such as fine cotton or silk. Synthetic materials are less

**Differing styles of blinds and curtains on the lift-off front of a large dolls' house. The elaborate curtains and blinds are made of Indian silk. This house is larger than average and wallpapers divided by strips of border have been used to match the internal decorations. A more uniform scheme, using one wallpaper and matching curtains or blinds, will produce a better effect if the house is small.**

suitable as they are not so pliable. Even with silk and cotton there is a tendency for curtains of such short lengths to flare out. To reduce bulk at the bottom, dispense with hems and smear a thin line of all-purpose glue along the edge of the material to prevent fraying.

### Materials

- Fine fabric of your choice
- Matching sewing thread
- Narrow cotton tape
- Decorative braid
- Gilt string or ribbon (optional)

### Method

1. Cut the fabric slightly longer than the window itself (allow enough for secure fastening above and a little overlap beneath the window), and about one-and-a-half times the width required for the finished curtain. (There are two curtains to make for each window.)
2. Gather or pleat the top of the fabric by hand. Glue or sew the two curtains at each end of a piece of narrow tape or seam binding, measuring slightly wider than the window.
3. Glue the tape to the wall above the window, using all-purpose glue, so that the curtains hang down on either side.
4. Cover the tape with a pelmet made from a strip of decorative braid, glued to the wall over the curtain top.

**5**  The curtains can be finished with tie-backs for a more elaborate effect. Gilt parcel string or narrow, floral-patterned ribbon can be knotted invisibly behind the curtain.

# Blinds

Blinds give a pleasingly uniform appearance both to the inside and outside of a house front. In a very confined space, they are also neater than curtains.

Ruched blinds made of fine material can add an instant air of charm and elegance, and are not difficult to make.

**Simplicity itself: the ruched blinds soften the Georgian windows in my interior design shop.**

## Materials

■ Fine fabric of your choice (preferably silk)
■ Matching sewing thread
■ Strip of thin card

## Method

**1**  Cut the fabric to nearly double the width of the window and about 5in (127mm) deep.
**2**  Fold the fabric in half to make the depth approximately 2½in (64mm) and press in the crease. It is important that the fabric be used double, as it will be visible from outside the house as well as inside.
**3**  Pleat the material into horizontal folds (four or five will be enough) and crease firmly (*see* diagram 1).

**Simple ruched blinds.**

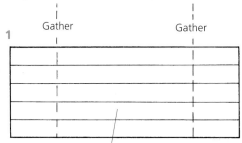

**4**  Catch stitch in two parallel rows (*see* diagram 1) then tighten and secure the thread (*see* diagram 2). This will gently shape the fabric, pulling it in and up.
**5**  Carefully flare out the ends.
**6**  Glue the blind to a ½in (13mm) deep strip of card and glue this in place over the top of the window, so that the bottom half of the blind overhangs the windowpane.

# Carpets and rugs

A miniature carpet or rug in complementary colours can provide just the right appearance of comfort to a dolls' house room. Needlepoint carpets made exactly to 1/12 scale are collectors' pieces, however. The finished articles tend to be prohibitively expensive for most pockets, and only the most dedicated professional miniaturists are capable of working on fine silk gauze to this scale with accuracy. Fortunately, charts and kits are available (at sensible prices) which are not so demanding for the average needlework enthusiast. Most people will happily settle for a rug worked on a canvas size of 18 or 22 count (stitches to the inch). This will be perfectly acceptable in the dolls' house and will not be too much of a strain to work.

If you would like to design your own dolls' house carpet rather than rely on a shop-bought kit, draw out your pattern on graph paper, remembering that one square equals one stitch on the canvas. The original nautical

This carpet was worked from a charted design for a dolls' house carpet. I used only the central portion of the design on a plain background and finished with the border pattern. The simpler effect often looks more convincing than a complicated pattern if you are working on a canvas size larger than strict 1/12 scale.

design featured in the picture on page 36 was made for the sea captain's house by a man who had never attempted needlework of any kind before, but thought it would be interesting to try. As you can see, it worked well, so be adventurous and have a go.

Half-cross stitch will produce a smoother effect than tent stitch (particularly if you are using a canvas count smaller than 18), and there will be less bulk at the back of the work. On 18 or 22 count canvas I would use one strand of Paterna Persian Yarn or two of stranded cotton or stranded tapestry wool. To finish off, turn under the edge of the canvas and oversew through the double thickness. To back the carpet, cut a piece of lightweight, iron-on dressmaker's interfacing slightly larger than the carpet and trim neatly after it has been ironed in place.

A professionally made cross stitch carpet which measures only 4¼ x 2in (108 x 51mm) worked on fine canvas. This charming design would suit a Georgian or Victorian room.

# 13 *Furniture*

There is a huge variety of furniture with which you could fill your dolls' house. You may wish to concentrate on collecting professionally crafted 1/12-scale miniatures, or you may be happy with less expensive and plainer ready-made furniture.

If you would rather save money and spend more time, then why not make your own furniture? It need not be complicated. Excellent kits are available now, offering furniture in a wide choice of styles, and they will be a good starting point for the beginner. Alternatively you can add a personal touch and make each item from scratch, from inexpensive materials you are quite likely to have around the house.

This chapter offers advice on assembling kits and then goes on to set out instructions for making various simple items of furniture. Practising on these pieces will give you an idea of what can be done without previous experience. As your skills in working with miniscule components improve, you can try out a few more tricky and sophisticated pieces.

## Making furniture from a kit

Assembling a piece from a kit is really the best way to begin making furniture. Wooden kits are designed by professional craftspeople to be made up by the amateur and are not intended to be a test of skill. If you are unable to fathom out the instructions, however, it may

seem like one. The following hints may not appear in the manufacturer's instructions, but if you take note of them now, you should avoid a certain amount of frustration while assembling the kit.

1   First check the parts. Lay them out on a tray and make sure every piece is there. Very tiny parts can all too easily fall out and be lost if you are not careful. It is a good idea to clear both the working surface and the surrounding area before you open the pack, so that you can spot that tiny piece of wood or metal which might otherwise never be found again.

2   Read the instructions right through and familiarize yourself with the parts and the order in which they must be assembled. You may not be able to follow the complete sequence immediately. Read the first steps through until you have a fair understanding of how the parts fit together and do not attempt to understand the next stage fully until you have completed the previous one. Once you have a rough idea of the sequence, the details should fall into place as you work.

3   Most kits will specify the type of adhesive to be used if it is not supplied, and whether the components should be painted or varnished before or after assembly. Remember that if you leave surplus glue on wood, you will not be able to varnish or polish over it later. Keep some white spirit handy and wipe off any tiny spots from the surface immediately.

You will also find the white spirit useful for removing glue from your fingers.

4    Masking tape is more useful than clamps or rubber bands for keeping small pieces together while glue is setting, and it can be peeled off easily later on. Masking tape is reusable: wind the used tape round an empty cotton reel and it can then be used again several times.

5    When the instructions say 'keep square', make sure that you do so. Find a small box round or into which you can fit the piece or, failing that, make a stiff cardboard shape to use as a mould, checking with a set square that the corners are accurate.

6    Do not hurry. If the instructions say 'allow to dry and set' before the next stage, you must do so, otherwise you may risk pushing the piece out of alignment or damaging it.

7    Rub over with fine glasspaper and wipe clean before you polish, paint or varnish. A good finish is all-important: it would be a pity to spend time carefully assembling a kit, only to spoil it in the later stages.

## Metal kits

Metal is sometimes used for kits, especially for small accessories where the parts are so tiny or intricate that it would not be possible to make them in wood (*see* the fireplace grate in the picture on page 97, for example). Here are a few practical tips for their assembly.

1    Metal kits for small accessories are inexpensive, but they are sometimes supplied without instructions. It can be daunting to be faced with a pile of unidentified bits of metal when you open the pack. There will be a picture of the finished miniature, however, and with patience you can work out from this how it all fits together. If possible, have a 'dry run' before gluing anything in.

2    Smooth down the parts before assembly: remove all nobbles with a file and then slightly roughen the places to be joined before applying epoxy resin as the adhesive.

3    Paint with primer or undercoat and finish

with model paint, followed by a coat of clear varnish.

4    For an intricate kit where several different paint colours are used, it is worth investing in a magnifier which can be hung around the neck on a cord (available from an optician, or a haberdashery department), so that detailing will be 100% accurate. A magnifier on a stand will be even better and easier to use, and will have many other uses for the miniaturist.

# Making furniture from scratch

When you have gained some experience by assembling a few pieces of wooden furniture from kits, you may like to try making something of your own. The materials needed for the two simple wood-based projects given below are inexpensive and easy to come by. Following these are ideas and instructions for making a variety of other pieces of furniture, none requiring complicated techniques or costly materials.

## Simple shelves

I made the shelves shown in the picture to fit a specific space in one of the rooms of my interior design shop. By following the method given here you can make your own shelves to

The shelves are spaced to accommodate a collection of miniature glass of different sizes.

whatever size you need to take particular books or ornaments.

I did cheat a little by making up an elaborate broken pediment from a kit to make my otherwise simple shelves look more impressive. You could leave them plain, or add decoration of your own. The bookshelves should be painted after assembly, but if you wish to varnish them instead, this should be done before gluing the parts together.

## Materials

- Plain stripwood, ½in (13mm) wide
- Matchsticks
- Wood moulding (optional)
- Broken pediment kit (optional)

## Method

1  Measure stripwood to the height required for the shelves and cut one piece for each side.
2  Decide on the number and width of shelves required and cut these from stripwood. Measure carefully: these pieces will fit in *between* the uprights.

**How to fit the bookshelf components together.**

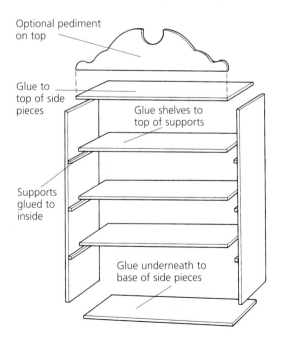

Optional pediment on top

Glue to top of side pieces

Glue shelves to top of supports

Supports glued to inside

Glue underneath to base of side pieces

3  Cut one piece of stripwood for the top and one piece for the base of the shelves. These pieces will be glued on later to *cover* the ends of the uprights so they must be slightly longer than the shelves.
4  Cut shelf supports from matchsticks (or very thin stripwood). Measure the spaces carefully and glue at intervals down one side of each upright. Check that they are spaced identically on both sides, or your shelves will not be straight.
5  Glue the shelves on top of the supports, securely butted up against the uprights on either side. Finally glue on the top and base.
6  For extra decoration if desired, finish the base and sides with wood moulding and the top with a broken pediment.

## Cutting identical shelf lengths

To measure identical lengths of wood for shelves, cut a pattern from stiff card to the required length. Use this as a guide when cutting each shelf: do not cut the first one and then use that to mark out the others. The width of even a thin pencil line will affect the measurement in the miniature scale. Cut exactly on the pencil mark each time.

# Aga cooker

The method below describes how to make a single-oven Aga for a small kitchen. Based on a wood block, the cooker is not hard to make and the finished article will look solid and satisfactory, even if the doors and hot-plate covers are fixed and do not open. If you are a stickler for every detail and want one with moving parts, there are kits available, made of plastic resin, for single- and double-oven models (*see* picture, page 18).

## Materials

- 1 block of wood, or small, rigid box – suggested dimensions: 3½in (89mm) long, 2½in (64mm) high, 1¾in (44mm) deep
- Dressmaker's hooks and eyes, or similar
- 2 metal washers

- 2 domed metal screw covers from mirror fixing screws
- Thick card or oddments of wood veneer
- Gloss model paint in one of the traditional Aga colours (white, dark green, red, cream or deep blue)
- Black gloss model paint
- Aga logo and thermometer strip, cut from a magazine advertisement (optional)
- A piece of thin metal rod (optional)

**When the Aga is painted, the surface resembles the enamel finish on a real Aga. Who could detect the humble materials from which it is made?**

### Method

1. Cut three pieces of card for the doors and glue them in place on the front of the wood block. (*See* the picture and diagram 1 for the arrangement and shapes of the doors.)
2. Glue the dressmaker's hooks and eyes to the doors to represent hinges and door catches. These will be painted over.

3. Undercoat the body of the Aga and topcoat in your chosen colour of model paint.
4. Cut a piece of card the same length as the top of the wood block and ½in (13mm) deeper. Score the card and bend the excess ½in (13mm) downwards to form a lip over the front edge (*see* diagram 2). Paint the card gloss black (including all the edges) and leave to dry before gluing on to the top of the Aga.
5. Cut a second piece of card the same length as the back of the wood block, and approximately 1in (25mm) higher, curving the top corners as shown in diagram 3. This will form the back of the Aga. Paint gloss black and leave to dry before gluing in place. There is no need to paint the lower part of the card, but remember to paint the top and side edges, as they will show.
6. Glue the two washers to the top of the Aga and cover with the metal domes.
7. If you have managed to find an Aga logo and thermometer strip in a magazine, glue this in place on the front (*see* picture).
8. Another option is to add a metal rail along the front. For the Aga in the picture I used the metal fastening pin from an old brooch.

# Screens

Screens are both decorative and useful, as they keep out draughts and can separate off different areas of a room. In a dolls' house there is no need to worry about draughts, but a screen can make an attractive accessory to a room. Following are details for making two different types of screen.

**Building an Aga cooker.**

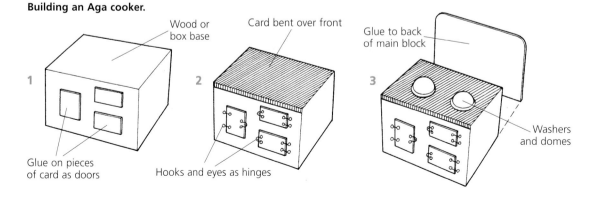

An instant screen: the concertina screen on the right can be made in fifteen minutes. For the 'Gothick' screen on the left, I copied an idea from the eighteenth century and used some of the print room wallpaper design on a yellow paper – the favoured background colour of the time.

## Concertina screen

A concertina is simple and quick to make, and is a perfect way to use up an unwanted piece of 1/12-scale wallpaper or border pattern.

### Materials

■ Coloured or patterned card (about half the thickness of mounting board: gift boxes are a useful source)
■ Wallpaper or wallpaper border, to suit the surrounding decor

### Method

1 Cut a rectangle from the card, approximately 8in (203mm) long and 5¼in (133mm) tall (or smaller if your room has limited space).
2 Cut out a matching rectangle of wallpaper and paste to the front of the card. Alternatively you could cut a smaller rectangle and surround this with a strip of border.
3 When the paste has dried out thoroughly, measure four equal sections on the card and score the back gently with a craft knife.
4 Fold the card into a concertina along the scored lines, pressing the sections together a few times to get the folds crisp and set in position.

## Hinged screen

This more sophisticated screen can also be plain and rectangular, but a rounded or pointed, 'Gothick' top on each panel adds interest and can make it more suitable for a variety of period interiors.

### Materials

■ Stiff card (mounting board) or thin wood
■ Dressmaking tape or seam binding
■ Fabric or wallpaper to suit the surrounding decor
■ Self-adhesive felt (available in small sheets to attach to the base of ornaments or lamps), or thick plain paper or fabric, preferably dark green
■ Narrow decorative braid (optional)

### Method

1 First cut a paper pattern in your preferred style (*see* diagram 1 for alternatives). For a round-topped screen the panels should be 6in (152mm) tall at the top of the curve. The 'Gothick' screen should measure 6¼in (159mm) at the point.

**Alternative patterns and construction for a hinged screen.**

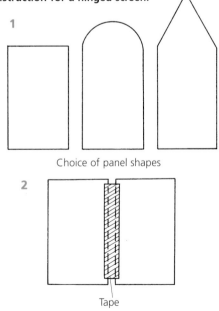

Choice of panel shapes

Tape

2   Fold the paper pattern in half lengthwise to check that any shaping is symmetrical and trim if necessary.

3   Using the paper pattern as a guide, cut out the required number of panels in the stiff card.

4   For a two-panel screen, make a tape hinge and glue to the back of the two panels as in diagram 2. For a three-panel screen, make a second tape hinge and glue to the front between the second and third panels.

5   Cut your chosen fabric or wallpaper to shape for each panel (again using the paper pattern) and glue to the front of the screen.

6   Cover the back of each panel with the self-adhesive felt or plain paper. If this is dark green, it can simulate the green baize traditionally used on the reverse of screens (the servants' side). Alternatively, choose a simple fabric or paper which complements the pattern on the front.

7   Edge with braid if desired.

# Seating

No house is complete without something for its residents to sit on. While there are any number of kits offering all kinds of seating, it can be fun to supplement these with a few home-made and comfortable items.

## Simple chair

Professionally made wooden chairs are expensive, as they require expertise, time and patience to construct. This simple chair is

**The red check material is actually a wide ribbon, while the patterned covering is part of some curtain border trim.**

armless and upholstered, and requires no woodworking skills to complete it.

- 1 cube of balsawood, approximately 1½in (38mm) square
- 2 pieces of thick cardboard, each 1½ x 3in (38 x 76mm)
- Dressmaker's wadding
- Cotton fabric (or curtain trimming), minimum width 3in (76mm)
- Thin braid or silk cord (optional)

**Method**

1   Fold one piece of the cardboard in half so that it measures 1½ x 1½in (38 x 38mm) when doubled over. Glue this to the back of the balsawood block, with the folded edge at the top. Tape round both the cardboard and the block with adhesive tape for extra strength (*see* diagram 1). The purpose of this is to give an extra thickness at the back of the chair seat, so that when the chair back is glued on, it will slope slightly backwards instead of being bolt upright.

**Constructing a simple covered chair.**

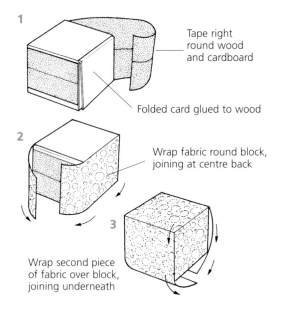

Tape right round wood and cardboard

Folded card glued to wood

Wrap fabric round block, joining at centre back

Wrap second piece of fabric over block, joining underneath

**2** Cut two pieces of fabric, each measuring 3 x 6½in (76 x 165mm). Fold each piece in half lengthwise and press.

**3** Glue one piece round the balsawood base (the seat) with the fold at the top, joining centre back with an overlap (*see* diagram 2).

**4** Glue the second piece of fabric over the balsawood base, with the folded edge at the front, joining underneath with an overlap at the centre of the base (*see* diagram 3). Make sure that this piece neatly covers the top of the first piece of fabric at the front.

**5** Cut a piece of wadding measuring 3 x 3in (76 x 76mm). Fold and glue this over the second piece of cardboard with the fold at one side and the edges meeting at the other (*see* diagram 4). This will form the chair back.

**6** Cut a piece of fabric 2¼in (57mm) wide by 6in (152mm) long and fold over the padded chair back with the fold going over the top and the raw edges at the bottom (*see* diagram 5). Turn in the edges neatly and sew down each side.

**7** Glue the chair back to the back of the seat (*see* diagram 6).

**8** As an optional extra, sew on some very thin silk cord or braid round the edges to trim.

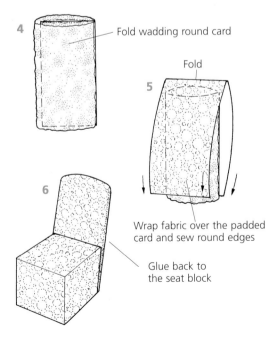

4 — Fold wadding round card

Fold

5

Wrap fabric over the padded card and sew round edges

6

Glue back to the seat block

---

### Checks

If you choose check fabric as your chair covering, take care to match the checks accurately at the joins.

## Pouffe

A pouffe is really a padded, comfortable variation on a basic wooden stool and can be used either as extra seating or as a footstool. A 1930s or '40s house would not be complete without one.

**The fabric covering for my pouffe is a thick cotton. A thinner braid would be more accurately to scale, but I decided to use a scrap I already had and rather like the flamboyant effect. For a modern room, a leather-covered pouffe would be appropriate, and an old glove could be recycled to make the covering.**

### Materials

■ 1 cylindrical piece of foam rubber, approximately 1in (25mm) tall by 1¼in (32mm) in diameter (I found a conveniently sized piece in the top of a bottle of bath salts; an alternative would be a section of a large cork)
■ Fabric of your choice (perhaps a thick cotton)
■ Furnishing braid to trim
■ 1 small bead

### Method

**1** Cut two pieces of the fabric:
**a)** one circle about ⅜in (10mm) larger all round than the top of the foam rubber;
**b)** one piece the same height as the foam

rubber and long enough to go round it, allowing an extra ⅜in (10mm) as an overlap.

2 Snip the circle of fabric at intervals, making the cuts no more than ¼in (6mm) long. Apply a thin trail of all-purpose glue round the edge and glue the fabric on to the top of the foam rubber, bending over the side edges where snipped, to give a neat fit (*see* diagram 1).

**Making a pouffe.**

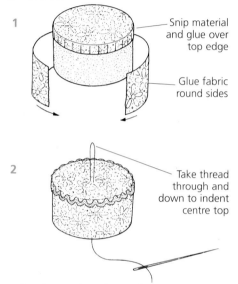

1 — Snip material and glue over top edge

— Glue fabric round sides

2 — Take thread through and down to indent centre top

3 Apply glue to the edges of the rectangle of fabric and glue this round the sides of the foam rubber, covering the snipped edges at the top (*see* diagram 1).

4 Cut braid the same length as the rectangle of fabric and glue round the sides to cover the join at the top.

5 Use a strong needle and thread (with a thimble) to go right through from underneath to the top of the pouffe. Take the thread back down and pull tight to create an indentation in the top (*see* diagram 2). Secure firmly with a knot at the base. Sew a small bead in the centre of the top to finish.

# Tables

Beautiful wooden tables can be made from kits, but sometimes it is good to soften a room with a covered or draped table. Two possibilities are included here.

**For the cloth on this table I used an embroidered mat, one of a set bought at a jumble sale. In a Victorian room, a deep red or green woollen fabric would look well. Blue-and-white check gingham would suit a modern setting.**

## Round covered table

An economical way of creating a round occasional table is to use a cotton reel as a base. The fabric covering it is the important part: no one will see what is underneath. Here is a method of doing this which disguises the cotton reel perfectly and prevents the fabric sticking out at an awkward angle. A very thin fabric will look just right if it flares out a little. Thin braid can be glued round the lower edge of thicker fabric to weigh it down.

### Materials

- 1 plastic or wooden cotton reel
- Firm card
- Dressmaker's lightweight iron-on interlining
- Fine fabric of your choice
- Thin braid (optional)

### Method

1 Cut a circle from the card, approximately 2½in (64mm) in diameter. A lid from a jam jar will provide a suitably-sized pattern. Glue the card to the top of the cotton reel, matching the centres (*see* diagram 1).

**A round table based on a cotton reel.**

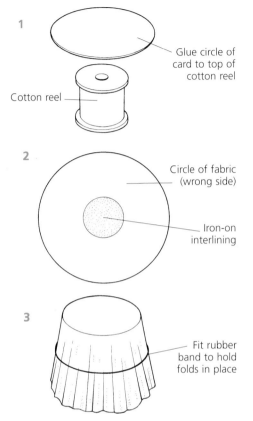

2   Cut a circle of fabric. The diameter should measure 2½in (64mm), plus twice the height of the table. A saucer or small plate might provide a pattern, or you could use a compass.

3   Cut a circle of interlining the same size as the card for the table top.

4   Match the centre of the fabric circle to the centre of the interlining circle and iron on (*see* diagram 2).

5   Mark the centre of the cloth with a pin and attach to the table top with double-sided adhesive tape or glue. The interlining will prevent either tape or glue showing through the cloth.

6   Spray the cloth with water until really damp, fit a rubber band round the sides and leave until completely dry to ensure that the cloth hangs in neat folds (*see* diagram 3).

7   If you wish, glue thin braid round the bottom of the cloth as a weight.

# Draped dressing table

A draped dressing table is a very old idea, but never seems to have gone out of fashion. Country house dressing tables have been draped in this way for two centuries. On a miniature scale, it is a good method of providing a pretty dressing table for a bedroom at minimal cost. Use lace for an elaborate effect, or sprigged cotton for a country cottage. The dimensions given below are only meant as a rough guide: there is no standard size for a dressing table and the measurements can be adapted to suit your room.

**The box used as the base for my dressing-table had a good finish and could be left just as it was; a block of wood will need to be painted before assembly if the table top is not to be covered.**

## Materials

■ 1 block of wood (painted if necessary) or rigid box – suggested dimensions: 4in (102mm) long, 2½in (64mm) tall, 1¾in (44mm) deep

■ 1 piece of thin wood, or strong card approximately 5in (127mm) tall and 4in (102mm) long

■ Fake mirror glass, or a small handbag mirror

■ Acetate

- Lace, or thin cotton fabric
- Ribbon trimming (optional)
- Coloured card (optional)

## Method

1   Glue the thin wood or card to the back of the base (the wood block or box), so that the top half extends above the base to form a back for the mirror (*see* diagram 1).

2   Cut a piece of 'mirror glass' to fit (it can be cut with scissors), then glue to the backing

**Creating a draped dressing table.**

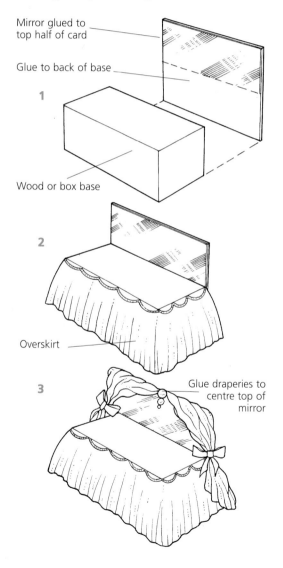

Mirror glued to top half of card

Glue to back of base

1

Wood or box base

2

Overskirt

3

Glue draperies to centre top of mirror

card above the table top. If you are using a miniature real mirror, you may need to adjust the measurements of the backing card to suit: it can be narrower than the complete width of the dressing table.

3   Cut an overskirt of the lace or cotton approximately 3in (76mm) high and 12in (304mm) long. Turn under ½in (13mm) along the top and tack or press in place. Gather the top edge to fit round the front and sides of the table. Arrange the gathers neatly, dab glue along the top and glue in place around the table (*see* diagram 2).

4   For the draperies round the mirror, cut another piece of the lace or cotton approximately 4in (102mm) high and 12in (305mm) long. Gather this into a ruched effect at the centre and fix to the top of the card-backed mirror (*see* diagram 3).

5   Arrange the drapes to fall on either side and fix back with ribbon bows (*see* page 98). Small artificial flowers or an old pair of clip earrings can also make decorative tie-backs for drapes.

## Peg dolls

While peg dolls are not exactly furniture, the techniques of dressing one up are not too dissimilar from those involved in the projects in this chapter. Peg dolls are ideal for children's dolls' houses but, suitably dressed, can equally well inhabit the more rarefied atmosphere of a collector's 1/12-scale house.

## Materials

- Old-fashioned wooden clothes pegs with round tops
- Pipe cleaners
- Scraps of fabric and lace trim
- Embroidery thread, stranded cotton or tapestry wool (for hair)

## Method

1   For a stand-up doll, saw off the rounded tips of the peg to make a straight base. For a sit-down doll, saw off the lower (divided) part of the peg (*see* diagram 1).

2   Wind a pipe cleaner round the body and

twist together firmly at centre back, fixing with a dab of glue. Tape round for extra security. Push the ends outwards to form the arms (*see* diagram 2).

3 For a sit-down doll, add a second pipe cleaner in the same way, at the base of the sawn-off peg, to form legs which can bend (*see* diagram 2).

4 Over-elaborate facial features can destroy the appeal of an otherwise charming doll: keep them simple. Use a fineline black pen and sketch in the eyes and mouth. Two small dots are all that is needed for a nose.

5 Make the hair in whatever style you want from the wool or thread, and glue in place.

6 To dress the doll, wrap a triangular piece of material or lace over the shoulders like a shawl to form the bodice and sleeves all in one piece (*see* diagram 3). Stitch under the arms to make the sleeves and secure the material back and front at the waist with a dab of glue. Add a gathered skirt and a ribbon sash to cover the join. A tiny hat or cap can be made from a scrap of lace edging.

### Drawing faces

It is best to draw the face first before you add hair, so that if you are not happy with your first attempt, you can try again on the other side and cover up your mistake.

**Making stand-up and sit-down peg dolls.**

1

Cut here for sit-down doll

Cut here for stand-up doll

2 Wrap pipecleaners round for arms and legs

3 Triangular material for bodice

**This peg doll is suitably dressed as an eighteenth-century nursemaid. Bows of narrow satin ribbon add a delicate finishing touch to the lacy drapes of the cradle.**

# 14 *Decorative detail*

Preceding chapters should have given you a head start on basic techniques for decorating and furnishing your dolls' house. This chapter sets out some more unusual decorative ideas and suggests a selection of ordinary items which are well worth seeking out and keeping safe. It is amazing what can be done in dolls' house scale with even the most mundane objects.

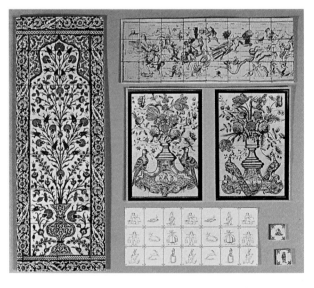

Blue-and-white tiles, whether real ceramic or fake, have many uses. Cards with tile designs make decorative panels (*see* the dairy pictured on page 25). A tile wallpaper design will suit a kitchen or a bathroom, and real ceramic tiles are the height of luxury for a grate surround (*see* picture, page 52). Shown above are a museum greetings card (left), tile panel pictures cut from magazines, tile-patterned wallpaper and miniature ceramic tiles.

## Paperwork

Paper and card are useful sources of imaginative effects for dolls' house interiors. It is worth salvaging anything you think looks interesting from packaging, greetings cards and giftwrap. Advertising leaflets, too, sometimes yield a tiny picture or an attractive border (*see* picture on page 64 – the border in the main room of my shop). Left-over wallpaper can be used to line shelves and drawers, or to make a screen (*see* page 87).

### Marbled paper

Marbled paper can be used instead of wallpaper (*see* page 61). It is also ideal for elegant fireplace panels and hearths (*see* page

Selected pictures of marble cut from glossy magazines and advertising leaflets. The black-and-white marble in the background is a photograph of a real marble surface, which I later used to make a floor.

50 and below). It can be used to make covers for miniature books: simply glue round a small piece of wood. Shiny marbled paper can be made into a table top, or even a whole floor if you have the right sort of house.

## The oriental look

Giftwrap with an oriental theme is perfect wallpaper for an eighteenth-century room. A Chinese-style picture from a magazine can be used as a wall panel, framed in wooden moulding.

This corner of the main room in my interior design shop is used to display classical furniture together with some Chinoiserie. The black-and-gold Chinese wall panels are framed in narrow stripwood, painted gold. The unusual surround above the fireplace was designed specially to show off the oriental painting of leopards, complemented by the pair of china leopards on the mantelshelf.

## Pictures

A room without any pictures in it always seems unfinished. Look around you, and I am sure you will see at least one picture on the wall, or perhaps a framed photograph or two on a table or desk.

Pictures complete a room setting in the dolls' house too – gilt-framed paintings in a Victorian parlour, tiny silhouettes in oval frames in a Regency house, or a bold and colourful work

An art gallery is the perfect way to display a selection of miniature paintings. This one is also beautifully lit inside, setting off the paintings to perfection.

in a wooden frame in a modern sitting room. Plan picture arrangements carefully to suit the style of the rooms.

Once you have decided on the type of picture which will complement your scheme, look out for small reproductions which will catch the mood of the period. Magazines are an excellent source of suitably sized pictures. The more expensive type of interior decoration magazine will have the best selection, as pictures are then printed on good-quality paper with the colouring exactly in register. Art and antiques periodicals will also offer a good yield.

Architectural prints hung over an elegant side table make an attractive group.

# Photocopying

Pen-and-ink sketches reduce well to miniature scale, and provide some variety from the more usual coloured pictures. I used a photocopier to miniaturize several sketches for a house with a William Morris theme.

The picture will need to be reduced several times in order to scale it down to the size you want, and you may find it useful to reinforce detail or thicken some of the lines at an intermediate stage. Each time the size is reduced, the picture will become darker and less clear, as minute patches of shading will show up where lines have merged and spoil the effect. Conceal the unwanted marks with liquid paper, so that the end result is a miniature sketch which is clean and sharp. This does take a bit of patience, but it makes a change from cutting every picture out of magazines.

This sketch by Edward Burne-Jones was miniaturized by using a photocopier and conveys all the charm and clarity of the original. It shows William Morris presenting an engagement ring to Janey, his wife-to-be.

# Framing

Small pictures can be framed to good effect in gilt jewellery mounts, which are designed to hold cameos or stones. Fake cameos cost very little and can be used as intended (see the cameos on either side of the fireplace in the picture on page 97). Inexpensive gilded frames complete with replica carving are also available in toy shops which stock children's dolls' house furniture.

Gilt jewellery mounts, here used to frame cameos and silhouettes, are inexpensive. I used a pair of rectangular, fake Wedgwood plaques as fireplace inserts (see page 95).

Pre-Raphaelite painter John William Waterhouse named this painting 'Spring'. All the fine details are included in this lovely miniature. Artists who specialize in miniature work can be commissioned to copy a favourite work of art and will also supply a suitable frame.

## Wooden frames

If you want to make your own wooden frames, you will need to use a metal mitre box and saw (see page 47) and 1/12–scale wooden picture frame mouldings. The mitred corners are cut in the same way as for fireplace mouldings (see page 49). Beware of dwarfing your picture with an outsize frame: framed pictures featured in magazines will give you an idea of the size of mouldings likely to be most suitable.

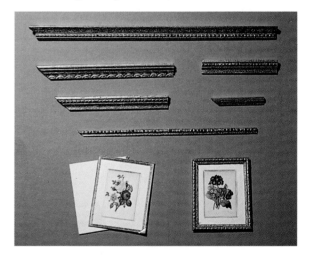

Choose simple or ornate gilded picture frame mouldings to complement the style of painting to be framed.

### Method

1   Cut out your chosen picture and glue on to a piece of fine white card, allowing a wide border all round. Use all-purpose

glue rather than paper glue, which could cause wrinkles.

2  Using a piece of wooden moulding as a guide, lay it in place along each side of the picture in turn and draw along it with a pencil to mark out on the card the finished dimensions of the frame. Trim the card to this size.

3  Cut the mouldings using the mitre box and saw. The opposite sides of the frame must be precisely the same length for a good fit. After cutting the first piece, mark the length for the second piece with a very sharp pencil before cutting. Repeat the process for the other two opposite sides.

4  Glue the mouldings around the picture on top of the spare card: smear each piece of moulding with all-purpose glue and leave until slightly tacky before fixing. This will avoid the danger of getting any glue on to the picture itself.

### Painted frames

Mahogany picture frame moulding needs no painting, but the edge of the backing card will need colouring to match, to avoid a white line showing. Use a felt-tip pen to colour the card neatly.

If you prefer gilded picture frames, paint the card edges, and the strips of moulding before cutting, and touch up the corners if necessary after gluing the frame together.

## Picture hanging

The way in which you hang pictures will enhance their impact. One large painting, fixed with a small dot of Blu-Tack at each corner, will look effective and imposing over a fireplace or in the centre of a wall. Take a tip from professional picture hangers and arrange smaller pictures in groups. Two or four prints of similar subjects hung close together make a better impact than assorted pictures spaced evenly around the room. The pictures also need to relate to any nearby furniture: try different arrangements, using a small blob of Blu-Tack, until you find the layout you like best.

**The colour scheme in this room is carefully co-ordinated. The Japanese print was mounted on pink card before framing; the spongeware on the mantelshelf adds the finishing touch.**

If the room has a fitted picture rail, suspend pictures from it with fine gilt string (glued to the rail and picture back). An alternative for a particularly ornate Victorian room is to attach a piece of thin brass rail to the wall with two eye-hooks (screwed into the wall). Hang the pictures from two pieces of gilt string (*see* diagram below). Glue beads on to each end of the rod as finials.

**Using a brass rail to hang pictures.**

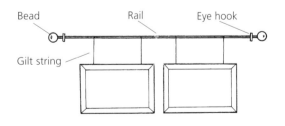

Small pictures in oval or round frames can be hung with a bow of thin velvet ribbon. A length of thin velvet ribbon with a bow at the top can also be used to suspend several small pictures in square or rectangular frames (*see* diagrams below).

**Suspending several pictures on a ribbon.**

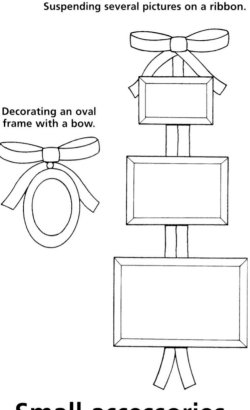

**Decorating an oval frame with a bow.**

# Small accessories

It is well worth starting to put together an oddments box of scraps of material, narrow ribbons, braids and lace trimmings, unusual beads or metal fastenings, and so on. Small items are never thrown away by a dolls' house owner. When you want to make anything new there is bound to be something handy in the oddments box which can be turned to miniature use.

My own bits box, which has evolved over many years, contains unusual buttons salvaged from long-gone clothing, wallpaper and fabric samples, gilt Christmas string and a whole pile of magazine cuttings with ideas I might want to adapt to small-size furnishing schemes at some later date. I keep old birthday and

Christmas cards with small designs, and even envelopes if the lining is an unusual texture or colour.

Here are some ideas. You will soon think of others once you are accustomed to looking at materials with 1/12-scale ideas in mind.

# Ribbons and cords

## Bows

A small-scale bow must be made up, not tied, in order to make it neat and flat. The following method should make a very fiddly process simple.

### Method

1   Cut a piece of ⅛in (3mm) wide ribbon to a length of about 2¼in (57mm). Fold in half, crease the fold, then fold in half again and crease the second fold. Using the creases as a guide, fold sides to middle and stitch in the centre (*see* diagram 1).
2   Cut a second piece of ribbon approximately ¾in (19mm) long. Fold over the centre of the bow and stitch at the back, folding in and overlapping one edge over the other (*see* diagram 2).
3   Cut a third piece of ribbon to a suitable length for the tie ends. Crease in the centre and stitch to the back of the bow (*see* diagram 2). Cut the ends at a slant.

**How to make a bow.**

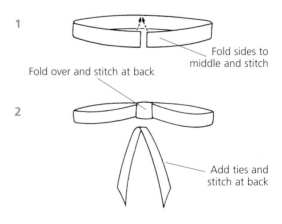

## Embroidered ribbon

Thin, embroidered or patterned ribbon will make a decorative bell pull to hang by the fireplace in a drawing room. Attach the top to a small brass ring and mitre the bottom edge (fold and sew the bottom corners back to form a point). Sew a small bead on to the point to finish.

**An exquisite Ribbon and Roses design bell pull, worked on silk gauze (40 holes per inch), is one of a selection available as a kit for those capable of such fine work. It can also be supplied ready worked.**

## Braid

Furnishing braid can make a very fine stair carpet, as it is usually thick enough to look suitably sturdy, but malleable enough to be fitted right to the back of the treads. Attach it with double-sided adhesive tape so that, if you want a change at any time, it can be removed easily.

## Piping cord

As an alternative to a plainer cornice, why not use white piping cord instead in a bathroom or seaside cottage?

## Silk cord

Very thin silk cord can be used for edging covered chairs, cushions and curtains, to add a finishing touch. Stitch it carefully and make sure it lies straight, or the effect will be spoiled (*see* picture of the chair on page 88).

## Lace

Lace edging is available in a huge range of widths and styles. The narrowest ones are suitable for edging dolls' clothing (*see* page 93). Picot-edged lace can be used to make a cornice. Extra-wide lace edging can be used for bedroom drapes (e.g. dressing table, page 91, and cradle, page 93).

# Buttons, beads and fasteners

### Buttons

Buttons can be used for all sorts of things around the dolls' house. A plain wooden button with a slight indentation makes a plate for the Tudor household. Fill it with fruit to hide the button holes. A metal button with a coat of arms on it makes an effective 'By Appointment' sign for a shop (*see* picture on page 61). The lion mask in verdigris paint finish, used as a wall ornament in my interior design shop (*see* page 61), is also a metal button. If you already have a box of miscellaneous buttons, look through it for inspiration. If you don't, start collecting now.

### Brass curtain rings

Small brass curtain rings come in handy as simple frames for round pictures. Back with card as for jewellery mounts and wooden frames (*see* page 97).

### Toggles

Cut the shaped ends from a wooden duffel coat toggle to use as feet for a bed (*see* diagram below).

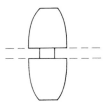

**Saw a wooden toggle to make feet for a bed.**

A bell-shaped plastic toggle with a hole in the top could make a lampshade for a (non-working) ceiling light in a modern house (*see* diagram below).

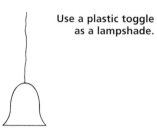

**Use a plastic toggle as a lampshade.**

## Earrings

Old clip earrings are just right for fastening back drapes or curtains in a grander room where simple ribbon or cord is not elaborate enough.

## Plant ties

One of the easiest ways to make evergreen house plants is to use wired green plant ties. Trim the edges to a leaf shape and bend to make an aspidistra or a fern.

No self-respecting Victorian home would have been without an aspidistra. The jardiniere is a suitable container for this easy to make plant.

## Beads

Like buttons, beads of all shapes and sizes can be put to good use in the dolls' house. Patterned macramé beads or unusual glass ones make perfect mantelshelf ornaments. A plain wooden bead can be transformed into a steamed pudding: tie the bead up in a piece of thin cotton or muslin, leaving the tie ends dangling, and place in a saucepan on the stove.

A large wooden bead can be used as the basis of a bay tree. Even if your dolls' house is not to have a garden, you can stand a bay tree on either side of the front door in terracotta pots, or you could use smaller ones as mantelshelf ornaments in a modern house.

### Materials

- 1 large wooden bead
- Pack of green flock powder (available from model railway stockists)
- Paper glue
- Plastic wood filler
- A real twig or a wooden cocktail stick

Topiary can be used indoors as well as outside. Miniature bay trees and a clipped yew can be made from wooden beads and a redundant chess piece.

1   Fill the centre hole in the bead with plastic wood filler and push in the twig or stick to form the trunk. Leave to set.

2   Brush paper glue on to the bead, hold by the 'trunk' and roll the bead round in the flock powder until well coated. You may need to repeat this process in order to cover the bead completely, but allow the first coating to set firmly before you do this. If any bald patches remain after a second coating of glue and flock powder, drip on a little extra glue and press flock powder into the bald spot with your finger.

3   Fix the bay tree in a small pot with Blu-Tack or wood filler and glue on a layer of sesame seeds to represent pebbles.

# Chess pieces

Old chess pieces are remarkably adaptable. If anyone in your family plays chess, they may have some spare, damaged pieces. Incomplete sets also turn up in jumble sales and at charity fairs, so it is worth looking out for them on the oddments stall. Chess pieces vary enormously in style, but the shapes shown here are the most common. Variations will also be suitable for most uses.

To make the accessories mentioned below, the pieces must be sawn off at strategic places. The best way to hold a piece steady while cutting is to use a mitre box and fix the piece in place with a large lump of Blu-Tack to keep it horizontal.

## Pawns

The tops of pawn pieces (*see* diagram below) make excellent finials for newel posts or small gates (*see* picture, page 99).

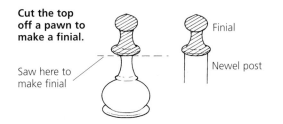

**Cut the top off a pawn to make a finial.**

Saw here to make finial

Finial

Newel post

## Knights

Paint two knights stone colour and use on either side of an imposing front door, or as gate piers for a large dolls' house. Black knights can be used in their entirety as finials for newel posts on Tudor or Jacobean staircases.

## Bishops, kings and queens

Saw off the top and use the body of the piece as a base for a topiary tree (*see* diagram below) using the same method with flock powder as for bay trees (*see* method opposite). These formalized trees can be used in the dolls' house garden or indoors (*see* picture, page 100).

The lower part of a king or queen will also make an attractively shaped urn (*see* below), which can be transformed with a painted verdigris finish or marbled effect (*see* page 69). A black piece could be left in its unpainted state to represent exotic ebony.

The base of any piece will make feet for a bed, stool or cupboard.

**Cutting guides on king, queen or bishop to make a topiary tree, an urn, or feet for furniture.**

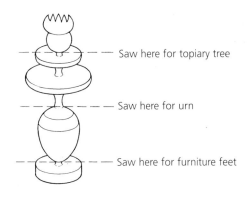

Saw here for topiary tree

Saw here for urn

Saw here for furniture feet

# Shell ornaments

Tiny iridescent shells can also be used in many ways. The smallest can be bought in packs; slightly larger specimens can be purchased separately. I have used shells in profusion in my interior design shop. As with beads, single shells make good mantelshelf ornaments. Brightly coloured ones look beautiful simply heaped in little baskets or arranged in tiny gilt shells (available in craft shops).

Use a small version of the real thing to create a decorative piece: these tiny shells appear identical in shape and colour to those which are twelve times the size.

## Shell picture frame

Glue tiny shells on to a wooden picture frame or mirror surround, arranging them in a colourful pattern. If the shells are really small, it is easiest to pick them up with tweezers. Superglue is the best adhesive to use.

## Regency shell box

Regency ladies were fond of covering boxes with patterns of shells, which were then varnished. I prefer to leave the shells in their natural state as varnish darkens them.

## Shell 'tree'

Another idea which became popular in the Regency period was to make trees out of shells. You need a small glass dome on a wooden base (available in dolls' house shops). Glue a twig on to the wooden base. Sort out your chosen shells into colours which will suggest those of flowers and glue them in place on the twig, building up the design to resemble a tree with blossom. This is painstaking, finicky work but, if you have the patience, the result will be something special. The finished tree should fit neatly inside the glass dome.

# 15 *Special shop details*

If you are fitting out a shop rather than a house, there are several specific items you will need to arrange, apart from basic decoration and contents as appropriate.

## Fascia boards

You can provide a suitable name for your shop in several ways. One method is to use a lettering stencil, which will give you a choice of type styles. The lettering can be outlined on a piece of card and coloured in using a gold pen or a black marker pen.

Another way to produce impressive lettering for a shop front is to use the self-adhesive gold

### Spacing letters

Take care when spacing stencilled letters. Look at some real examples first. Make base and top lines with masking tape so that your letters are in a straight line.

letters intended to personalize luggage. Attach the letters with Blu-Tack first so that you can adjust the spacing if necessary before fixing on.

For the many people who own or have access to a word processor and printer, the simplest option is to choose a suitable typeface from those available on the computer and set it in a very large font size. Make trial printings until you have a version which looks good when trimmed and held in place on the shop front.

**Not everyone is a talented signwriter, and providing a suitable shop fascia board sometimes causes problems. I have used stencilling and self-adhesive letters with success, but on this occasion my daughter and son-in-law, both graphic artists, gave me the shop name as a Christmas present.**

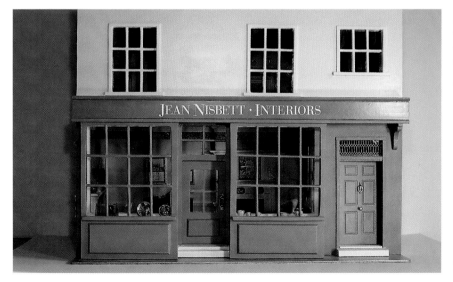

The window display of this curio shop is arranged to show off sparkling glass and ornaments, and looks equally enticing both from inside and outside the shop. The striped wallpaper and rope twist border framing the window help to establish the impression of a seaside souvenir shop.

For the final version, try to print it on a thin, shiny card or, failing that, on a shiny paper which must then be pasted on to card, trimmed to size and glued in place. Some printers will also print with black and white reversed, and colour printers add to the possibilities.

# Window displays

A good window display is vital in any shop: it is the first thing to catch the eye. Window dressing is a special skill. Next time you go shopping, study the displays and see what makes an interesting window rather than a dull one. You can give height to your arrangement by fitting shelves (adapt the method for simple bookshelves on page 85 as necessary). Small Perspex boxes make excellent display stands. Add a length of thin brass tube on which you can hang suitable miniatures.

# Shop bell

A traditional shop should have a bell above the door to alert the shopkeeper to customers. Attach a small bell just above the door, suspended from a hook by thin wire, so that it tinkles when the door is opened and closed. Don't forget to make an 'open' and 'closed' sign to hang on the door.

A hanging sign is a good way to attract custom. Attach a metal bracket to the wall with superglue. The sign can be handwritten, or it could be a picture.

### Realistic food

To make earthy potatoes for a green-grocer's display, model small, potato-shaped balls from modelling compound and harden in the oven in the usual way. Brush with glue and roll the potatoes in railway modeller's earth flock powder. Shake off the excess to give a natural look.

# 16 *Practical gardening*

If you have sufficient space, a garden, whether large or small, is a definite asset and added attraction to a dolls' house. Chapter 5 suggested some ideas and points to consider, and this chapter offers practical tips and techniques for bringing your planned garden into being.

Once you have decided on the layout of your garden or patio and the principal features you would like to include, make a plan on paper. Otherwise you could end up with too much crammed in, or some awkward gaps. Do not try to include too many features in a small space, or the result will be confused rather than restful. When you are satisfied with your plan, and know what you want, pay a visit to your nearest model railway stockist for some scenic materials.

**An espaliered tree against a brick wall is a space-saving idea in a tiny garden. A deckchair on the lawn completes the summery scene.**

## Creating a basic garden

Below is a suggested method for creating a basic garden. You can add to and alter this to suit your own ideas.

### Materials

- A piece of lawn grass – sold in a roll or by the piece
- Packs of coloured flock powder for earth, sand and gravel, plus green to make hedges
- Foliage in a variety of colours
- Stiff cardboard
- Baseboard (*see* page 32)

### Method

1. Cut out a piece of the cardboard to use as a base. This will be fixed on top of the baseboard with double-sided tape, so that it can be replaced easily at a later stage if you decide on any changes. Copy your plan on to the card for accurate guidance.
2. Cut out the lawns first, and try the pieces of 'grass' for size, working from your plan. Set them aside, to be glued in after the paths and borders have been laid, to avoid sprinkling them with flock powder.
3. Brush paper glue over the surfaces you have marked out as paths and sprinkle them with sand or gravel flock powder.

When the glue is dry, turn the card upside down over a sheet of newspaper and tap it a few times to shake off the surplus. Repeat the process to cover any bald patches.

4  Make the borders and flowerbeds with earth flock powder in the same way. They will look better if raised slightly by gluing in an extra layer of thick card or scrunched-up paper first.

5  Glue on the pieces of lawn.

# Additional features

## Terraces and paved paths

An alternative to sand or gravel paths is to lay paving. Sheets of 1/12-scale paving can be cut to fit your design (*see* cladding, page 55). Alternatively, you can make your own paving stones from stone-coloured modelling compound. Purchased flagstones in cast resin or ceramic are a further option for a terrace, although more expensive (*see* page 32).

## Plants

### Hedges

For a neatly trimmed hedge, use a strip of balsawood, about 1½ to 2in (38 to 51mm) thick, cut to the height you prefer. Gently curve the top edge with a craft knife, spread the balsawood with glue and sprinkle thoroughly with green flock powder. Tap off the surplus powder when the glue has dried, and re-apply if necessary to cover any bald patches.

### Trees

To make a natural-looking tree, use a twig as a trunk and glue on foliage (available in various shapes and sizes from model railway stockists). The foliage can be trimmed to any shape you want. If you want to make a more formal clipped tree, perhaps for a terrace or patio, follow the instructions for making an ornamental bay tree, given on pages 100–1.

### Creeper

A low wall on at least one side of the garden will make an excellent base for creeper. Make the wall from a strip of wood at the height you want, and cover with stone or brick cladding. Foliage, as for trees, can be cut to shape and glued in place up the wall.

### Flowers

Fill the borders and flowerbeds with colourful miniature flowers. I like to use a few choice specimens made by specialist craftspeople and make the rest myself from modelling compound. Dried flowers also look most effective, but will need changing frequently as they fade. If you spray them with hair spray after arranging, they will last longer.

## Garden pond

Use fake mirror glass (*see* page 108) to represent the water for a garden pond. Build up the edges into a raised bank by gluing on layers of paper or card, well covered with earth or grass flock powder, and arrange plants round the edge to disguise the join. Tiny real pebbles or 'rocks' (pieces of polystyrene packaging material, suitably painted) will also contribute to the attractiveness of the feature. Fix the 'rocks' with polystyrene cement. All other glues will dissolve this material.

## Garden buildings

Conservatories are available in all shapes and sizes (*see* pages 31, 33 and 107). You can buy one ready made, or assemble one from a kit, or you can adapt a mini-greenhouse from a home decoration store or garden centre, which will be even more economical. These are really intended for seed propagation and will not be so realistic as a genuine miniature made from a kit, as there is no door and the roof simply lifts off instead. It would, however, be an easy and economical way to begin: you can always 'upgrade' the structure at a later date.

When painting the woodwork, it is wise to use masking tape over any ready-fitted glass. I used white paint for my Edwardian version,

taken I had not finished, and have since added a trailing vine, complete with tiny grapes, inside the roof.

# Window boxes

If you do not have enough space to create a miniature garden or terrace, why not add a touch of colour by putting window boxes on the house itself? Alternatively, these little boxes can be fixed at ground level to represent a flower border (*see picture, page 110*).

Below **A window box along the front of this little shop is filled with artificial flowers (of the sort normally used to trim hats).**

Above **A lean-to conservatory, ready to decorate and fill with plants and flowers. This ready-built design has its own base and wall so that when decorated it can be placed directly against a house wall with no fuss.**

Below **A conservatory is the ideal spot to spend a lazy summer afternoon. The token garden roller in the corner was found on a junk stall: it is made of copper and brass.**

shown in the picture above. The floor is simply wrapping paper in a Pugin-style design, pasted down and covered with a thin sheet of acetate so that it looks like shiny tiles. I also added some frilly metal roof-ridging, fixed on with superglue, a miniature garden table and chair, and some plants. When this photograph was

## Materials

■ Thin stripwood about ½in (13mm) wide
■ White or green paint
■ Artificial flowers and/or foliage

## Method

1  Cut two pieces of stripwood to the length required (e.g. to fit the length of the window).
2  Cut two more pieces approximately ½ to ¾in (13 to 19mm) long to form the ends of the box.

**3** Glue together, taking care to fit the sides between the front and back lengths to make a neat front edge.

**4** Paint the box white or green.

**5** Fill with artificial flowers and leaves.

**6** Blu-Tack the boxes to the front of the house rather than fixing them in place permanently. This will make it easier to change the flower arrangement later if wanted.

# Japanese garden

Japanese gardens have a special tranquillity which is appealing to an increasing number of Westerners. I enjoyed making a small arrangement for myself on a balcony last summer and was so delighted with the result that I planned an even smaller version to attach to a dolls' house. My son adapted and extended my original design to make a setting for a tiny garden pavilion.

**This peaceful Japanese garden provides the perfect setting for an oriental building. Real evergreen foliage in the background adds to the natural effect, but will need replacing from time to time. An alternative would be to make a tree from a gnarled twig, with fake foliage glued on.**

## Materials

- Flat wooden box with a raised edge – I used one measuring 6¾ x 8½in (171 x 215mm) which had contained tablets of soap
- A piece of emery paper, grade 2½ (available from home decoration stores)
- Small black, white and grey pebbles
- A small pagoda or oriental-looking ornament (you may find just the thing among the ornaments sold as decorations for tropical fish tanks)
- Plastic plants intended for use in fish tanks
- Plasticine
- Green flock powder
- Fake mirror glass (optional)

## Method

**1** Cut the emery paper to fit inside the box. Leave it in its natural state for golden sand, but if you prefer a grey-white sand, paint it with very pale grey emulsion. Either is suitable for this type of garden.

**2** A traditional, simple garden designed for contemplation needs only a few shrubs and pebbles. These should be strategically placed, singly or in groups of odd numbers, such as three or five. In the true Japanese garden, groups of even numbers are considered unlucky.

**3** Cut the plastic water plants to the shapes you want and embed in a little mound of Plasticine. Brush the Plasticine with paper glue and cover with green flock powder to represent moss.

**4** A more elaborate garden can have additional features. Embed an ornament in a Plasticine base as for the plants, or make a small pond from fake mirror glass, disguising the edges with moss or small shrubs.

**5** For a natural scenic effect, arrange a pile of stones in one corner.

**6** A simple bridge over a pond can be made from several thin strips of wood, stained and glued together with a very thin strip added as a simple handrail.

**The arrangement of the garden is simplicity itself.**

# 17 *Renovation*

Interest in old dolls' houses has increased with the growth of the hobby. This is often the starting point for someone who still has the house with which they or their children played, and the idea of renovating an old favourite can be very tempting.

A dolls' house which has been handed down through more than one generation in a family may be a genuine treasure, and it is wise to check when it was made. Consult your local museum curator or a dolls' house magazine for an opinion: send a photograph in the first instance.

Another point to consider is whether the house is a candidate for conservation, restoration, or renovation, as each option will require a different level of work. A beautifully made Victorian or Edwardian house which has been neglected would still be appreciated enormously by a collector, and would lose much of its value if radically altered. Collectors enjoy houses with the original wallpapers and paintwork, even though these may be in poor condition. Such a house would simply need careful cleaning, preferably by an expert.

If the house is not of sentimental value to you, why not put your small property on the market, buy a new dolls' house with the proceeds, and make a fresh start? Restoring a rickety old house demands considerable time and patience, and you may find that starting again from scratch will be more satisfying.

If you have some decorative ideas you would like to try out before beginning on a new dolls' house, an old house could provide a useful practice ground.

An old home-made dolls' house is another candidate for restoration, and here you need to take a close look and ask yourself, 'Is it really worth it?' If the house is badly made from poor quality wood, or infected with woodworm, and the architectural style is of no known provenance, however much care and attention you lavish on updating it, you will probably remain unsatisfied with the results. Again, it might be better to channel your energies into new work.

The picture below shows just such a house after renovation, as an example. This

**It was impossible to improve this roughly-made house to anything approaching beauty, and disguise was the only answer. Crooked window frames are covered with stripwood and lace curtains soften the overlarge plate glass windows. I covered the glass with masking tape when painting the windows. Despite all its faults, this house offered great pleasure and many games to two young children.**

obviously home-made house has an ugly facade, and oddly shaped windows fitted with heavy plate glass. I used it as a practice piece when I first began, so it was useful in that I learned how to construct a new roof (the old one was missing) and was able to try out all sorts of decorative effects inside.

The most commonly available house for renovation is a Triang, or one of its contemporaries. Various brands of commercially-made dolls' houses were produced in large numbers from the 1920s to the 1960s, all made in 1/16 scale. They have a nostalgic charm, particularly for anyone who played with one as a child. More often than not, the original wallpaper will be in tatters and too far gone to keep. I prefer to restore this type of house to something approaching its original appearance so that it can be enjoyed by a new generation of children. If you prefer the faded, period look, then all you can do is to clean the house thoroughly and leave well alone.

**This flat-roofed Triang house is neat and trim after renovation. The metal sliding front now moves easily and the ledge at the base provides a small space for a few flowering plants.**

# Hints on cleaning before redecoration

1   Give the house a careful scrub from top to bottom. Watch out for any nails left sticking up. This is a messy job, so work outdoors if possible. Remove old wallpaper by wetting it thoroughly: leave for a few minutes and use a scraper. Leave the house to dry in the open air or by a window.

2   Traces left by carpeting that has been glued firmly in place can be difficult to remove. Although the carpet can be pulled away fairly easily, it may leave a sticky residue on the floor. If hot water alone does not work, try different solvents on small patches until you find one that makes an impression. It will be a matter of trial and error and guesswork. White spirit often works well. If the glue really will not come off, it will simply have to be covered up with a new floor covering – or you may be able to sandpaper the marks away.

3   Sometimes an old house will have been painted in unsuitable colours with gloss paint, itself an inappropriate finish. Use a proprietary brand of paint-stripper and wire wool, in a well-ventilated room or, preferably, outdoors. Always wear rubber gloves when using paint-stripper.

4   Rub over with glasspaper until the surface is smooth and wipe it over with white spirit to leave a really clean surface for redecoration.

# Points to watch

## Roofs

The roofs on most of the Triang era houses were made of thick cardboard, layered firmly together and coloured red. The corners were very vulnerable and you may find that the layers have separated and some of the cardboard is missing. The simplest approach is to cut new sections of similarly weighted cardboard and fit and glue them in to make the corners up to the right thickness. Try to match the original colour of the roof by mixing a similar shade with acrylic paint (*see* page 73).

## Metal sliding fronts

Some Triang houses had sliding metal fronts, which may have become battered over the years. If you have one of this type, try to straighten out the bent metal as much as possible. The metal is quite soft, so do not use a hammer because it may do more harm than good. Careful and patient bending by hand is the best method. Make sure that the front runs smoothly in the grooves at the top and bottom. Clean the grooves carefully, then use a candle to wax the runners until the front will slide easily to open and close.

## Front door and windows

Triang, Romside and Gee Bees houses all had metal front doors and windows with lattice panes. These were also sold separately for the dolls' house builder. It is still possible to obtain replacement doors and windows in the correct scale from some hobby shops and mail order outlets, although they will now be made of plastic, not metal. For a home-made house you will probably need to custom-build a wooden door to fit the doorway.

**This Gee Bees house needed attention to both roof and window frames, but otherwise was in reasonable condition when bought in a street market. For the windows, cream paint makes a more pleasing contrast with the blue than the original bright yellow, and new glazing is a great improvement. The windows now all open easily and after repair, which included fitting a new roof ridge (*see* page 73), the roof was entirely repainted with acrylic paint.**

## Painted exteriors

Most Triang houses had flowers painted directly on to the front walls to provide a token garden – hollyhocks were the most favoured species. When renovated, a plain house can be enhanced by something similar, if your painting skills are good enough. A window box or two, or some flowers or creeper around the front door would also be a simple way of livening up the front in a fresh way (*see* page 107).

## The interior

If you have taken the trouble to renovate an old dolls' house, you probably have firm ideas on how you want the interior to look. Alternatively, if you are more interested in conservation and restoration and want to keep the period look of, say, a 1930s Triang house, it is worth bearing in mind the preferred colour schemes of the day. The wealth of interior decoration ideas and possibilities available today simply did not exist, and many houses tended to be uniform inside (*see* page 14 for ideas on colour schemes).

## Furniture

It is not easy to find furniture in the correct 1/16 scale to suit these older houses, but occasionally pieces turn up in antique markets and at some miniatures fairs, where old as well as new pieces are included. Professional miniaturists make replicas of furniture in various sizes and, if you choose carefully, you may be able to find some which will be of a reasonable size for your house. If you make some of the things I have suggested earlier, remember to scale them down slightly.

# Bibliography

**Agius**, Pauline, *Ackermann's Regency Furniture and Interiors*, The Crowood Press, 1984

**Bath City Council**, *Bath Shopfronts: Guidelines for Design and Conservation*, Department of Environmental Services, Bath City Council, 1993

**Beard**, Geoffrey, *The National Trust Book of the English House Interior*, Viking and Viking Penguin Inc. N.Y., 1990

**Benson**, E. F., *Mapp and Lucia*, Heinemann, 1967

**Davidson**, Caroline, *The World of Mary Ellen Best*, Chatto & Windus, 1985

**Glasgow School of Art**, *Charles Rennie Mackintosh*, Richard Drew Publishing, 1987

**Hockman**, Hilary, *Edwardian House Style*, David & Charles, 1994

**Innes**, Jocasta, *Exterior Details*, Collins & Brown, 1990

**Miller**, Judith, *Period Fireplaces*, Mitchell Beazley, 1995

**Nash**, Judy, *Thatchers and Thatching*, Batsford, 1991

**Parissien**, Steven, *The Georgian Group Book of the Georgian House*, Aurum Press, 1995

**Oster**, Maggie, *Japanese Garden Style: Eastern Traditions in Western Garden Design*, Quarto, 1993 (hardback), Cassell, 1994 (paperback)

**Sperling**, Diana (watercolours) and **Mingay**, Gordon (text), *Mrs Hurst Dancing and Other Scenes from Regency Life*, Victor Gollancz Ltd, 1981

**Swindells**, David J., *Restoring Period Timber-framed Houses*, David & Charles, 1987

**Wilhide**, Elizabeth, *William Morris Decor and Design*, Pavilion, 1991

**Woodforde**, John, *Georgian Houses for All*, Routledge & Kegan Paul, 1978

## Further reading

**Cole**, Christopher, *Make Your Own Dolls' House*, Van Nostrand Reinhold N.Y., 1976 (and London, Shepheard-Walwyn)

**Granger**, Janet, *Miniature Needlepoint Carpets*, GMC Publications, 1996

**King**, Patricia, *Making Dolls' House Furniture*, GMC Publications, 1991

**Lodder**, Carol and Nigel, *Making Dolls' House Interiors*, David & Charles, 1994

**McBaine**, Susan, *Needlework Designs for Miniature Projects*, Dover Publications Inc. N.Y., 1984

**Percival**, Joyce, *Architecture for Dolls' Houses*, GMC Publications, 1996

**Sorensen**, Grethe, *Needlework Designs from Oriental Rugs*, Charles Scribner's Sons N.Y., 1983

# Dolls' house magazines

## Britain

*Dolls House and Miniature Scene*
(monthly; on general sale or by subscription)
EMF Publishing
7 Ferringham Lane
Ferring
W. Sussex BN12 5ND
Tel: 01903 244900
Fax: 01903 506626

*Dolls' House World*
(monthly; on general sale or by subscription;
also published in Japan in translation)
Ashdown Publishing Ltd
Avalon Court
Star Road
Partridge Green
W. Sussex RH13 8RY
Tel: 01403 711511
Fax: 01403 711521

*International Dolls' House News*
(monthly; on general sale or by subscription)
Nexus Subscription Service
Tower House
Sovereign Park
Lathkill Street
Market Harborough
Leics LE16 9EF
Tel: 01858 435344 (credit card order line)

## United States

*Miniature Collector*
(bi-monthly; by subscription)
Ruth M Keessen Publisher, Scott Advertising
& Publishing Co
Scott Publications Dept NO33
30595 Eight Mile
Livonia
MI 48152-1798
Tel: 1-800-458-8237
Fax: 810-477-6795

*Nutshell News*
(monthly; by subscription)
Kalmbach Publishing Co
21027 Crossroads Circle
PO Box 1612
Waukesha
WI 53187
Tel: 1-800-533-6644 (subscriptions)

## Netherlands

*Poppenhuizen & Miniaturen*
(quarterly; by subscription)
Postbus 84
5384 ZH Heesch
Holland
Tel: 04125 2331

**NB**: Telephone numbers given here are for
calls within the country. Add international
dialling codes as appropriate.

# Metric conversion table

## Inches to millimetres and centimetres

mm – millimetres        cm – centimetres

| inches | mm | cm | inches | cm | inches | cm |
|--------|-----|------|--------|------|--------|-------|
| ⅛ | 3 | 0.3 | 9 | 22.9 | 30 | 76.2 |
| ¼ | 6 | 0.6 | 10 | 25.4 | 31 | 78.7 |
| ⅜ | 10 | 1.0 | 11 | 27.9 | 32 | 81.3 |
| ½ | 13 | 1.3 | 12 | 30.5 | 33 | 83.8 |
| ⅝ | 16 | 1.6 | 13 | 33.0 | 34 | 86.4 |
| ¾ | 19 | 1.9 | 14 | 35.6 | 35 | 88.9 |
| ⅞ | 22 | 2.2 | 15 | 38.1 | 36 | 91.4 |
| 1 | 25 | 2.5 | 16 | 40.6 | 37 | 94.0 |
| 1¼ | 32 | 3.2 | 17 | 43.2 | 38 | 96.5 |
| 1½ | 38 | 3.8 | 18 | 45.7 | 39 | 99.1 |
| 1¾ | 44 | 4.4 | 19 | 48.3 | 40 | 101.6 |
| 2 | 51 | 5.1 | 20 | 50.8 | 41 | 104.1 |
| 2½ | 64 | 6.4 | 21 | 53.3 | 42 | 106.7 |
| 3 | 76 | 7.6 | 22 | 55.9 | 43 | 109.2 |
| 3½ | 89 | 8.9 | 23 | 58.4 | 44 | 111.8 |
| 4 | 102 | 10.2 | 24 | 61.0 | 45 | 114.3 |
| 4½ | 114 | 11.4 | 25 | 63.5 | 46 | 116.8 |
| 5 | 127 | 12.7 | 26 | 66.0 | 47 | 119.4 |
| 6 | 152 | 15.2 | 27 | 68.6 | 48 | 121.9 |
| 7 | 178 | 17.8 | 28 | 71.1 | 49 | 124.5 |
| 8 | 203 | 20.3 | 29 | 73.7 | 50 | 127.0 |

# About the author

Jean Nisbett began to take notice of period houses, their decoration and furniture before she was ten years old, and they have been a consuming passion ever since. While bringing up a family she turned this interest to the miniature scale, and restored, decorated and furnished many dolls' houses. Her houses have been shown on Channel 4, BBC Television and TF1 France.

She began writing while working in the London offices of an American advertising agency, and is well known as the leading British writer in the dolls' house field. Her articles have appeared regularly in specialist miniatures and dolls' house magazines since 1985, as well as in home decoration magazines. This is her third book for GMC Publications. She lives in Bath, Somerset.

# *Index*

# TITLES AVAILABLE FROM
# GMC PUBLICATIONS

## BOOKS

## WOODWORKING

| | | | |
|---|---|---|---|
| 40 More Woodworking Plans & Projects | GMC Publications | Making Little Boxes from Wood | John Bennett |
| Bird Boxes and Feeders for the Garden | Dave Mackenzie | Making Shaker Furniture | Barry Jackson |
| Complete Woodfinishing | Ian Hosker | Making Unusual Miniatures | Graham Spalding |
| Electric Woodwork | Jeremy Broun | Pine Furniture Projects | Dave Mackenzie |
| Furniture Projects | Rod Wales | Security for the Householder: | |
| Furniture Restoration (Practical Crafts) | Kevin Jan Bonner | Fitting locks and other devices | E. Phillips |
| Furniture Restoration for Beginners | Kevin Jan Bonner | Sharpening Pocket Reference Book | Jim Kingshott |
| Green Woodwork | Barry Jackson | Sharpening: The Complete Guide | Jim Kingshott |
| Incredible Router | Jeremy Broun | Tool Making for Woodworkers | Ray Larsen |
| Making & Modifying Woodworking Tools | Jim Kingshott | Woodfinishing Handbook (Practical Crafts) | Ian Hosker |
| Making Chairs and Tables | GMC Publications | Woodworking Plans/Projects | GMC Publications |
| Making Fine Furniture | Tom Darby | The Workshop | Jim Kingshott |

## WOODTURNING

| | | | |
|---|---|---|---|
| Adventures in Woodturning | David Springett | Practical Tips for Turners & Carvers | GMC Publications |
| Bert Marsh: Woodturner | Bert Marsh | Practical Tips for Woodturners | GMC Publications |
| Bill Jones' Notes from the Turning Shop | Bill Jones | Spindle Turning | GMC Publications |
| Bill Jones' Further Notes from the Turning Shop | Bill Jones | Turning Miniatures in Wood | John Sainsbury |
| Colouring Techniques for Woodturners | Jan Sanders | Turning Wooden Toys | Terry Lawrence |
| Decorative Techniques for Woodturners | Hilary Bowen | Understanding Woodturning | Ann & Bob Phillips |
| Essential Tips for Woodturners | GMC Publications | Useful Woodturning Projects | GMC Publications |
| Faceplate Turning | GMC Publications | Woodturning: A Foundation Course | Keith Rowley |
| Fun at the Lathe | R.C. Bell | Woodturning Jewellery | Hilary Bowen |
| Illustrated Woodturning Techniques | John Hunnex | Woodturning Masterclass | Tony Boase |
| Keith Rowley's Woodturning Projects | Keith Rowley | Woodturning: A Sourcebook Of Shapes | John Hunnex |
| Make Money from Woodturning | Ann & Bob Phillips | Woodturning Techniques | GMC Publications |
| Multi-Centre Woodturning | Ray Hopper | Woodturning Wizardry | David Springett |
| Pleasure and Profit from Woodturning | Reg Sherwin | | |

## WOODCARVING

| | | | |
|---|---|---|---|
| The Art of the Woodcarver | GMC Publications | Understanding Woodcarving | GMC Publications |
| Carving Birds & Beasts | GMC Publications | Wildfowl Carving - Volume 1 | Jim Pearce |
| Carving on Turning | GMC Publications | Wildfowl Carving - Volume 2 | Jim Pearce |
| Carving Realistic Birds | David Tippey | The Woodcarvers | GMC Publications |
| Decorative Woodcarving | Jeremy Williams | Woodcarving: A Complete Course | Ron Butterfield |
| Essential Tips for Woodcarvers | GMC Publications | Woodcarving for Beginners | GMC Publications |
| Essential Woodcarving Techniques | Dick Onians | Woodcarving: A Foundation Course | Zoë Gertner |
| Lettercarving in Wood | Chris Pye | Woodcarving Tools, Materials & Equipment | Chris Pye |

## UPHOLSTERY

| | | | |
|---|---|---|---|
| Seat Weaving (Practical Crafts) | Ricky Holdstock | Upholstery Restoration Projects | David James |
| Upholsterer's Pocket Reference Book | David James | Upholstery Techniques & Projects | David James |
| Upholstery: A Complete Course | David James | | |

## TOYMAKING

| | | | |
|---|---|---|---|
| Designing & Making Wooden Toys | *Terry Kelly* | Making Wooden Toys & Games | *Jeff & Jennie Loader* |
| Fun to Make Wooden Toys and Games | *Jeff & Jennie Loader* | Restoring Rocking Horses | *Clive Green & Anthony Dew* |
| Making Board Peg & Dice Games | *Jeff & Jennie Loader* | | |

## DOLLS' HOUSES

| | | | |
|---|---|---|---|
| Architecture for Dolls' Houses | *Joyce Percival* | Making Georgian Dolls' Houses | *Derek & Sheila Rowbottom* |
| Beginners' Guide to the Dolls' House Hobby | *Jean Nisbett* | Making Period Dolls' House Accessories | *Andrea Barham* |
| The Complete Dolls' House Book | *Jean Nisbett* | Making Period Dolls' House Furniture | *Derek & Sheila Rowbottom* |
| Dolls' House Bathrooms - Lots of Little Loos | *Patricia King* | Making Tudor Dolls' Houses | *Derek & Sheila Rowbottom* |
| Easy to Make Dolls' House Accessories | *Andrea Barham* | Making Victorian Dolls' House Furniture | *Patricia King* |
| Make Your Own Dolls' House Furniture | *Maurice Harper* | Miniature Needlepoint Carpets | *Janet Granger* |
| Making Dolls' House Furniture | *Patricia King* | The Secrets of the Dolls' House Makers | *Jean Nisbett* |

## CRAFTS

| | | | |
|---|---|---|---|
| Celtic Knotwork Designs | *Sheila Sturrock* | Embroidery Tips & Hints | *Harold Hayes* |
| Collage from Seeds, Leaves and Flowers | *Joan Carver* | Introduction to Pyrography (Practical Crafts) | *Stephen Poole* |
| Complete Pyrography | *Stephen Poole* | Making Knitwear Fit | *Pat Ashforth & Steve Plummer* |
| Creating Knitwear Designs | *Pat Ashforth & Steve Plummer* | Tassel Making for Beginners | *Enid Taylor* |
| Cross Stitch Kitchen Projects | *Janet Granger* | Tatting Collage | *Lindsay Rogers* |
| Cross Stitch on Colour | *Sheena Rogers* | | |

# VIDEOS

| | | | |
|---|---|---|---|
| Drop-in and Pinstuffed Seats | *David James* | Classic Profiles | *Dennis White* |
| Stuffover Upholstery | *David James* | Twists and Advanced Turning | *Dennis White* |
| Elliptical Turning | *David Springett* | Sharpening the Professional Way | *Jim Kingshott* |
| Woodturning Wizardry | *David Springett* | Sharpening Turning & Carving Tools | *Jim Kingshott* |
| Turning Between Centres | *Dennis White* | Bowl Turning | *John Jordan* |
| Turning Bowls | *Dennis White* | Hollow Turning | *John Jordan* |
| Boxes, Goblets & Screw Threads | *Dennis White* | Woodturning: A Foundation Course | *Keith Rowley* |
| Novelties and Projects | *Dennis White* | Carving a Figure - The Female Form | *Ray Gonzalez* |

# MAGAZINES

### WOODTURNING · WOODCARVING · TOYMAKING
### FURNITURE & CABINETMAKING · BUSINESSMATTERS
### CREATIVE IDEAS FOR THE HOME · THE ROUTER

The above represents a full list of all titles currently published or scheduled to be published. All are available direct from the Publishers or through bookshops, newsagents and specialist retailers.

To place an order, or to obtain a complete catalogue, contact:

**GMC Publications,**
**166 High Street, Lewes, East Sussex BN7 1XU United Kingdom**
**Tel: 01273 488005  Fax: 01273 478606**

*Orders by credit card are accepted*